*To those who have already found solace in their flowers and those on the way to finding it.*

# Flowers
for Friends

JULIA ATKINSON-DUNN

KOA PRESS

Roadside buttercups keeping me company in my home office.

# CONTENTS

# FOREWORD

Over the last 10 or so years I have followed Julia's journey through her design blog 'Studio Home', and I have been delighted to watch from the sidelines her love of flowers, gardening and floral arranging grow. Julia's way with words left an indelible mark on me and I have always been inspired by her relatability, her honesty and her down-to-earth grace. Instagram gave us an easy way to stay connected and up to date with what we were both doing and I've thoroughly enjoyed Julia's first book, *Petal Power*. This year I made the exciting decision to return to Aotearoa after 20 years abroad and I knew that Julia would be a kindred spirit when it came to flower life back home. Flower friends do tend to remain close regardless of distance.

•

*Flowers for Friends* struck a chord with me instantly; there is a humanity to this beautiful work. The book speaks to honouring the seasons, connecting us to time and place. It gives clear uncomplicated technical guidance without any fuss or steadfast rules. I love the practical basics as well as the romantic and whimsical. It is clear in these pages that Julia finds not only joy but a sense of healing and grounding in gardening and flowering and there is such a spirit of generosity in the way she shares this.

•

My own floral career spans 25 years and I've witnessed the unique power and magic that flowers hold. Cecilia Fox, my florist business of 15 years, has always been guided by the fleeting beauty of the ever-changing seasons, and at its heart is a love of the natural world. Capturing the moments of growth and abundance as well as celebrating wilting and decay.

•

The way in which we relate to flowers, I think speaks to our yearning for a closer connection to the natural world. There is something intoxicating about flowers that often grows and intertwines into an obsession. While flowers alone can conjure deep emotions and nostalgia, the act of arranging flowers holds a potency all of its own. As a career florist, often working under extreme time pressures and tight budget restraints, it is easy to get caught up in the production of flowering for others, and to find yourself focusing on the dollar value of each stem. I was once asked in an interview if I found myself in meditation when arranging flowers and at the time baulked at the idea! I was busy! I was stressed and most definitely not in meditation. Perhaps I've softened this year or perhaps that question triggered something inside of me. Now I know the true joy that can be found in gathering and arranging flowers for ourselves, for our home and for our loved ones.

•

*Flowers for Friends* is an invitation back to our natural world, and to ourselves. Julia's joyous way with flowers, and her friendly words and images have created a book that is charming and breezy. A book that captures all the moments we hold close when it comes to flowers and how we orchestrate them in the garden and in the vase. Whether you are an aspiring florist or an inspired gardener, *Flowers for Friends* is so much more than a 'how-to' book – it's a true expression of the delight and the unencumbered joy that flowers can bring to our everyday lives.

•

*Melanie Stapleton – Cecilia Fox*

Previous page: A cheerful mix of dahlias and foraged lupins. Above: A detail of 'Shrine to Delphi' (page 76).

# "*Before I disappeared into full gardener mode, I was a flower thief.*"

Despite my former disinterest in growing them, cut flowers and foliage were always in my life. From the rescued petunias my toddler sister stamped on, to the pressed herbs I filed away in a scrapbook while investigating options for being a witch, even at a young age I took joy from items plucked from the garden. The kitchen table was never without its central, colourful vase from the garden and trips to the city sometimes involved stopping at the cemetery to lay little home-grown posies to past family.

•

Living in Auckland as an adult I found it difficult to not swipe offerings that hung over fences and I often screeched to a halt for side-of-the-road missions to collect rosehips in Central Otago. Bringing these fleeting natural moments into the house to take up residence by my desk or bed is a ritual that has always been with me, but it wasn't until I started growing plants myself that I realised it was a ritual that fed my happiness.

•

Within the pages of this book, I hope you find inspiration and encouragement to open your eyes to the weird and wonderful specimens that you too might be able to experiment with. Whether you are a gardener yourself, an enthusiastic forager or someone who enjoys a trawl of their mum's borders, there is calm, refuge and creativity to be found in arranging.

•

I have joked about my passion for flower arranging as being incredibly old-fashioned. That unless you are a florist it kind of sounds like an older person's sport. What I have come to realise is that our lives have sped up, our home plots are smaller and taking 30 minutes out of a day to gently rove with secateurs in hand can seem frivolous. All the discussion around mindfulness and self-care seems to rest in meditation apps, exercise and face masks. Yet, the time I spend harvesting and arranging imperfect home-grown stems to be enjoyed for a fleeting moment, is one of the most impactful things I have done for my own wellbeing.

•

This is also a book about flower arranging from the perspective of a gardener. Harvesting from the garden means short and wonky stems, bruised petals, insects crawling out of blooms and the open invitation to claim a weed or vege as vase fodder. Unlike the demands that florists are under to produce perfection, we at home are only out to please ourselves, or if they are lucky, our friends.

*Julia x*

# BRINGING YOUR GARDEN INDOORS

A CASUAL APPROACH TO GATHERING, PREPARING
AND ARRANGING HOME-GROWN OR FORAGED STEMS.
THE JOY IS IN THE PROCESS.

**Previous page:** Julia at her home in Christchurch, New Zealand, finding a spot for her 'Rubies & Raspberries' arrangement (page 156).
**Opposite:** Freshly harvested summer blooms from the garden.

# HOME ARRANGER'S TOOLKIT

## MY ESSENTIAL ITEMS

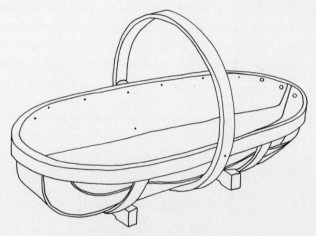

### Bucket or trug

Some arrangers may choose to harvest with a bucket of water at hand to promote better longevity of blooms. I find a flower trug to be the most user-friendly for gently piling up what I collect.

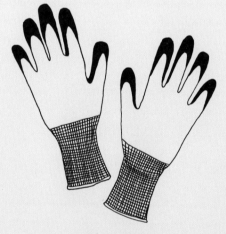

### Gloves

Really only vital when dealing with brutal spiky roses or thorny branches.

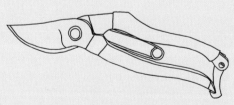

### Secateurs

Buy well and buy once. Invest in a quality pair of strong secateurs that can cleanly slice through woody stems. Needed for the harvesting of branches and thicker stems such as dahlias and sunflowers.

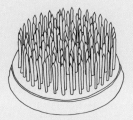

## Flower frog

Also called a needle cushion, pin holder or kenzan, it is a weighted support that sits at the bottom of a vessel allowing you to pierce stems into it for positioning. These can be used alone or in tandem with chicken wire.

•

A further handy addition would be using a waterproof adhesive putty (like museum wax or florist-specific putty) to secure the flower frog in place.

•

Keep an eye out in second-hand shops and in your family's back cupboard for older options. They can be expensive to buy and it's very handy to have a collection of different sizes.

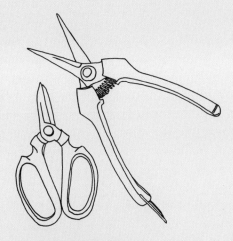

## Slim-nosed or florist-specific snips

For harvesting delicate stems and conditioning flowers once inside, I prefer to use smaller, slim-nosed snips that help to be precise. I also enjoy lightweight, florist-specific snips for recutting stems while arranging.

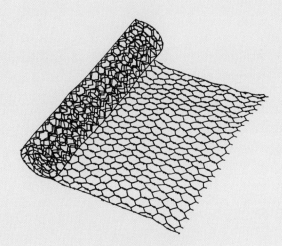

## Chicken wire

Chicken wire is a terrific, user-friendly alternative to traditional floral foams which are harmful to the environment. You will be trimming this down to size for different vessels, so some wire cutters are handy too! Easily found at hardware stores, I prefer the plastic-coated option but straight wire is fine.

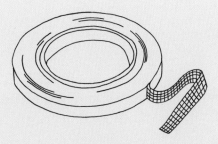

## Pot tape

Easily sourced online from floral design stores, this tape is stretchy and water resistant, allowing you to create grids across the top of a wide-necked vessel to both support stems and keep chicken wire from popping out. It is available in green or clear to help it hide within the foliage.

# HARVESTING

## TIPS FOR GATHERING FROM YOUR GARDEN

The aim, when gathering, is to avoid destroying the beauty of your garden scape for the sake of an arrangement. It is all about compromise. I long ago moved on from the lust for pristine, commercial-length stems, as this too often meant sacrificing establishing buds. I'm not fussy about wonkiness. I will leave flowers on the plant to enjoy outside before harvesting for the vase, knowing they may have only a few days left in them.

Typically, I don't head out to the garden with an arrangement in mind, instead letting the size and mix be dictated by the stage of flowering that I can access. It's about finding the balance and the best of both worlds that you have curated.

It is also about looking beyond traditional cut flowers. Where my gone-to-seed parsley used to be a frustration, I have discovered the flowers are a terrific, strong green filler in arrangements. Occasionally, I even make a truce with my rampaging clover, nipping some perfect leaves to add to a tiny bedside posy.

Sidelining the odd drop of strawberries, raspberry cane or lemon branches from the table feeds my soul in different ways when displayed for some whimsy. Seed heads present a whole new vibe and even roadside weeds offer incredible colour and joy when rescued from the untended wilds!

It is important to remember that harvesting flowers will motivate most plants to generate new growth. Harvesting is just like deadheading or pruning, but you undertake it a little earlier to enjoy the blooms inside as well. Annuals like sweet peas and cosmos, along with perennials like echinacea, rudbeckia and scabiosa take cutting as real encouragement, often extending their flowering period.

## Time your harvest

During the heat of summer, it is best to harvest flowers in the early morning or after dusk. Despite your best efforts, thirsty, hot blooms can wilt quickly once cut. Look for strong, turgid stems to show plants are well hydrated before picking.

## Think before snipping

For soft-stemmed plants, use sharp snips to cut on a 45-degree angle just above the junction of a branch or leaf node (see below). In most cases, plants will then generate new growth from this point for you to enjoy later in the season. When choosing where to cut, I try to achieve usable stem length without sacrificing too many new buds or offshoots of new growth.

For roses and hydrangeas, use strong secateurs to cut chosen stem on a 45-degree angle just above the junction of a leaf. When selecting the length, the most important thing to do is to make sure you leave plenty of leaves still on the stem to enable the plant to flourish again.

For tree branches and shrubs with woody stems, I try to make my cut at a junction with another branch to avoid stubby, sawn-off limbs where possible.

Opposite page: Loading the trug on a summer's day. Top right: Hellebores shown with stamens and in more mature form with central seed pod. Above: When harvesting, snip closely above a branch, leaf or bud intersection.

## Get to know them

As a gardener you will learn the optimal time to harvest from each plant. For example, it is best to pick snapdragons when only the lower flowers start to open. The same can be said for other spire blooms such as foxgloves and veronica. However, delphiniums need most flowers open before picking! Only time and practice will help you learn these individual quirks.

**Some of my top tips include:**
- Fennel flowers need to be acidic yellow/green before picking to avoid wilting.
- Hellebores (above) are very sulky in the vase, and last much longer if you wait to cut when there is at least one bloom on the stem that has developed a central seed pod.
- Roses are best when the outer petals of a bloom have opened, however leaving the flowers to fully open to enjoy on the bush for a while before cutting works well too, they just have a shorter vase life.
- Dahlia buds will not open in the vase. Pick once blooms are mostly or fully open.
- Bearded irises commonly have two or more blooms on one stem. I've discovered that harvesting when the first bloom is open will still allow for the buds to open in the vase too, I simply just snip the dead one off.
- The flowers of echinacea, cosmos, veronica, geums, bog sage and many other green-stemmed annuals and perennials are best harvested once the flowers have been open for a few days. I find they often collapse, almost instantly, if harvested when super fresh.
- Harvesting every open flower from your sweet pea vines 1–3 times a week will maximise new growth. It seems harsh but continuing to prevent any seed pods forming will vastly extend your flowering season.

# CONDITIONING

PREPARATION MAKES ALL THE DIFFERENCE

Home-grown blooms are beautiful in their imperfection. Bruised and nibbled petals, strangely developed heads and disease-touched leaves are all part of it. There is much you can do with polishing them up during the conditioning phase, but equally, the focus should remain on the calm time spent handling them and the satisfaction in growing these creatures yourself. You aren't selling your work, just filling your cup.

I readily pluck the dying collar off an otherwise perfect dahlia bloom, shaking out the earwigs at the same time. I don't worry about missing Japanese anemone petals and simply scrape off the lower,

shrivelled heads of snapdragons to enjoy the pristine ones at the top. Nature doesn't wait for us; be happy with what she offers.

## Hydrate hard

If you aren't harvesting with a bucket of water, you need to plunge your stems right up to their necks in clean water as soon as possible. Fill the sink or use water-filled vessels to support them, ensuring they are all submerged. If time allows, it's a great idea to let them hydrate for a few hours or even overnight before arranging.

**Above:** Garden-gathered stems having a drink in the sink.

## Strip

This process is about preventing the water from rotting. Either as you hydrate or as you arrange, work through your stems and remove all leaves or buds that will sit below the waterline. Return to the water ready for arranging later or pop straight into your vase. As you arrange you might choose to remove more leaves to reduce bulk where needed and snip off any diseased ones. Don't be afraid to pluck off petals that don't please you too.

## Cut

Tree branches, woody stems of roses and hydrangeas should be cut on a 45-degree angle to desired vase length, then again, with a vertical cut up the stem before placing in a vase. This allows increased surface area to draw water.

## Sear or score

Once cut to your desired length, poppies, hellebores and other floppy plants benefit from dipping the bottom 10 per cent of their stems into freshly boiled water for 20–30 seconds before arranging. This helps to seal the cut and prevent folding. Do not recut the stem after searing.

Another option is to skip the searing for hellebores and instead score down the lower half of the stem using a sharp blade (see above), opening it ever so slightly to allow more water in.

## Separate

Some plants need special treatment. Sappy plants like daffodils and euphorbia should be isolated in water from others to allow the stem fluid to dispel. This allows the stem to heal before mixing with other plants and avoids contaminating the vase water. Do not recut before adding to the vessel.

# ARRANGING

## APPROACHES TO HELP DEVELOP YOUR STYLE

As my passion for the garden grew, so did my appetite for learning about arranging. I have signed up to courses, inhaled Instagram demonstrations and read guide books spanning 60 years. What I have come to discover is that I enjoy building my own arrangements without the bounds of a set recipe that might threaten the easy-going, creative process.

Garden-grown stems are sporadic in length, quality and availability, essentially guiding your placement as you go. With lots of play time I have developed my own casual style and techniques that result in an end product that I can enjoy without the weight of achieving perfection. Find comfort in the whimsy as this is simply an appreciation of your own growing efforts.

**Above:** Mid-arranging of 'Pink Lemonade' (page 124). **Opposite top:** A mishmash of available flowers, breaking the rules of balance and including the little guys. **Opposite bottom:** A simple but joyful gathering of Iceland poppies.

# PREPARATION

## More is more

When harvesting I select as many different flowers and bits of foliage as I can. A wide variation of shapes and colour will really enhance a home-made posy. If it is an abundant time of year, I might have fun selecting complementary tones to create a cohesive story, or if things are sparse, I simply collect everything available and enjoy the natural, diverse chorus they create. Your home-made arrangements are a true reflection of the season outside.

## The one-woman show

Alternatively, when time is low and you are rich with one particular plant type, find a suitable vase – and spotlight it. There is both a feeling of simplicity and luxury when things are displayed en masse and the same can be said for plants.

The winding stems of Iceland poppies (below), Japanese anemones and bog sage look wonderful displayed this way, as do hydrangeas and tree branches. I just love bringing wintery branches inside to force their buds to blossom in the warmth of the house. Equally, I enjoy doing the same with the acid green of leafy spring growth or the heated tones as they crackle and sink into autumn.

In all instances, I do my best to get as much length as possible to produce a dramatic display not always achievable with flowers.

## Use what you can get

A common recommendation in achieving balance in an arrangement is to highlight your feature flower types by using them in odd numbers. For example, three roses, five rudbeckia or 15 shasta daisies amongst supporting foliage and smaller flowers. However, the garden doesn't always allow for this and I simply gather up what is ready and available. If I scrounged two roses and a single dahlia, so be it.

## Don't overlook foliage

Leafy limbs offer great opportunities to inject colour, texture, support and abundance into your arrangements. Some of my favourite foliage I collect to use from my garden belongs to aquilegia, thalictrum and pittosporum.

## Remember the little guys

Don't overlook the shorter-stemmed, dainty and delicate blooms. Wispy or just tiny flowers can help add bulk and interest to a medium or large arrangement. If their stems are too short to support themselves, I will thread them in at the end, balanced on the surrounding sturdier flowers and always making sure their toes still reach the water.

My favourite minis are nemesia, forget-me-nots, matricaria, knautia, Mexican daisies, lobelia and pansies. Although they can be fiddly to condition, they are a lovely supporting act or can be arranged together into a tiny vase for a shelf.

## Flowers *then* vase

Select your vase based on the appearance and number of the flowers you have at hand. This is where my collection of multiple vessels comes in handy. Forcing stems into a vase that is too tall or too roomy for your selection will have a disappointing visual result. Consider this permission to grow a collection of options!

## Be supportive

Set yourself up for easy, enjoyable creating by bringing in some support. In wider-necked vessels, bowls, compotes or troughs, make life easier by utilising flower frogs, chicken wire, pot tape or all three.

**1. Flower frog**

I find these particularly handy in my little vases that won't accommodate chicken wire but have wider openings. They really help support those first five or so stems that will then, in turn, support others threaded in. Blindly, you will be spiking ends onto the pins or squeezing them into the spaces and it might take a few goes to find the right position. Flower frogs could also be used alone, in a shallow, water-filled dish to create loose little stands of flowers.

**2. Chicken wire**

A curled-over pillow of chicken wire, squeezed into a wide-necked vessel is a game changer for home arranging.

**My top tips for using chicken wire:**

- Guestimate the width of the opening of your vessel and double this to cut a square of chicken wire with equal sides. Use appropriate wire cutters to avoid destroying secateurs!
- Roughly curl under each corner to meet in the centre, catching the ends together to form a pillow-type shape. You can then curl and bend this inward to squeeze into your vase.
- When using chicken wire, pay special attention to snipping off any thorns or branches from your stems that might catch as you thread them in and out.
- With bulbous-style vases or jugs, I find that the lip around the rim tends to hold my chicken wire ball well and there is no need for tape.
- With bowls and troughs, you will quickly discover that the weight of any stems will likely pop it out; this is when your pot tape comes in handy.
- Once your flowers have died, simply untangle from the ball, give it a good scrub and stow it back on the shelf with the vessel it was formed to fit.

**3. Pot tape**

Stretch lengths of your thin, waterproof pot tape across the opening of your vessel, pulling over the sides about 2–3 cm and cutting with sharp scissors. Depending on the size of your vase you should aim to criss-cross and create a grid across the top with four or more strips. As you build your arrangement you can play with stems to drape over the sides and hide the tape around the edges.

Opposite top: Using the longer stem of a peony to decide the appropriate height of the arrangement. **Opposite far right:** Mapping out the overall shape of an arrangement using foliage or structural stems. **Opposite bottom left:** 'Season of the Soul' (page 120) arranged to be positioned with its back against a wall.

# PROCESS

## Getting started

In my experimentation I have adopted a few differing techniques when approaching the building of an arrangement. This begins with visualising the scale in relation to the vessel, followed by where I plan for it to be displayed.

### 1. Stem height vs vase height

While this is not always possible, I try to loosely follow the rule that my overall arrangement will be 1–1.5 times taller and bigger than the vase it is housed in. I consider this when taking into account the possible height that can be achieved with the stems I have, followed by which vase would be suitable to enable this balance. If unsure, hold the stems up to your vase selection to work out the best match.

### 2. Where will it be seen

When arranging, you have the choice to create in reflection of how the vase will be viewed. I often make up vases that are 'party at the front, business at the back', as I know I will be displaying them on a mantelpiece against a wall. If you are making an arrangement to be viewed from all sides (360 degrees), make sure you regularly turn the vase as you build, creating a balanced spread of stems. This doesn't mean it is totally spherical, just that there is interest and viewing comfort from all points.

### 3. Handling stems

To get in the flow, simply hold each stem against the vase and emerging arrangement to gauge not only placement but the length you trim the stem to before threading into the vase. A fresh cut promotes greater ability to suck up water for better vase life.

### 4. Keep it casual and off-centre

As a home arranger, I have found it easier to create with asymmetry and looseness in mind. This gives the just-picked vibe and steps away from any comparison with pristine, traditional arrangements. To achieve this, I often aim to have my tallest bloom off to one side, and balance this with a lower trailing or swooping accent on the opposite side. This has a natural see-saw effect. Flowers are given space to breathe and be seen, particularly around the edges and top line of the arrangement.

### 5. Mapping the shape

Using foliage or my most voluminous plant type, I add stems to create an overall outline of what I want the arrangement to follow. From here I continue adding stems, usually working from the most to least of each plant type I have, commonly leaving my smallest and daintiest stems until last so they don't get squashed. This method works particularly well for arrangements that might be sitting with their back against a wall, viewed only from the front and sides.

*"Remember these guides are not hard and fast.
Be prepared to pull everything apart and start again! It's not
a job, it's enjoyable experimentation with nature's creatures."*

### 6. Outside in

With this method, beginning again with foliage or the most voluminous stems I have, I thread around the rim of the vessel, before slowly building up and inward. This method works particularly well when making an arrangement that will be viewed from 360 degrees, common to central table settings.

### 7. Go with the flow

Wonky, wayward and curly stems cannot be negotiated with! Simply hold the bendy stem against your developing arrangement, see where its natural swoop would fit best and thread it in.

Remember these guides are not hard and fast. Be prepared to pull everything apart and start again! It's not a job, it's enjoyable experimentation with nature's creatures.

## Prolonging vase life

The easiest and best way to keep your arrangement happy is to top its water up daily. To keep it fresh for even longer, emptying and refilling with fresh water is best, but far too complicated with larger arrangements that you have used support in. I have watched and listened to all manner of advice around adding life enhancers to the water and conclude that fresh is simply best.

You will note that flowers decay at different speeds. Don't hold back on pulling out dead stems or even plucking off wilted petals (above) to leave interesting nude bobbles. This is a favourite trick I do with tired echinacea, rudbeckia and Japanese anemones; finding their seed heads as captivating as the full bloom.

Sometimes you will strike a plant that outlives every other it is sharing a vase with. Set it aside, freshly snip its stem and rearrange with new friends from the garden. I regularly do this with fennel, honeysuckle, *Verbena bonariensis* and astrantia.

**Top left:** Using stems of honeysuckle to begin arrangement in a jar. **Bottom left:** Working with, not against the natural bends of wisteria and tree lupin. **Opposite:** My kitchen spice shelf is a revolving still life reflecting the seasons. Featured here are heleniums, cosmos, bog sage, *Sanguisorba officinalis,* scabiosa, poppy seed heads and echinacea with petals removed.

# ARRANGING THROUGH THE SEASONS

It was only after I started making a garden that it occurred to me I had lost touch with the seasons. I'd forgotten the magic of autumn light, the volatility of spring weather and the incredible transformation that perennials track through on a yearly basis. This reconnection to nature's cycle has unexpectedly brought me some balance to the pressures of daily life and unpredictable world events. While my own garden cracked open this door for me, I've realised the seasonal shifts can be found and plugged into by anyone with a window or a walk to work. Noticing the seasonal march forward of the earth is an option for everyone, gardener or not.

Growing, harvesting, foraging and bringing seasonal treasures into the house also isn't reliant on a big space, just a ready pair of snips and prioritising some time to slip out of the weekly rush.

With all seasons, calendar months are unable to concretely define the ebb and flow of Mother Nature, but for the sake of this book, I am sharing my arrangements by dividing them into the months that I collected them.

In line with the Southern Hemisphere's seasonal shifts, spring examples were made from September to November, summer ones between December and the end of February. Autumn, with its heat in March, ending with crispiness in May and the still, wintery finds from June through to August.

As all arrangements are gathered locally by me in Canterbury, New Zealand, you may find the timing of your own regional conditions differs to the monthly guides I have used here.

That is nature for you!

# SPRING

Of all the seasons, spring gets my blood pumping. The smell of cut grass is like a garden aphrodisiac, pulling me back outside on the daily watch for new growth and rewards. Flirting with the temperature gauge, it distracts with the staggered arrival of blossom then slams in with a devastating late frost.

In its earliest arrival spring teases with ripening buds, crisp mornings and a slow warming for lunch to be eaten outside again. While so many of my favourite early plants surprise us in the leftover breath of winter, they come charged with the exciting promise of the seasonal beauties to follow.

When I think of springtime in my own garden, it is daffodils, outrageously fragrant narcissi, jasmine and a carpet of cherry blossom. Every year I diligently chip away at my autumn-sown sweet pea vines, forcing their continued flowering and bundling together frothy posies for neighbours, visitors and quite often, people walking past the front gate! Where winter made me hunt for flowery treasures, the warmer spring mornings offer new pickings every day.

As the freshness of those earlier months starts to melt into the mildness of summer, tulips, aquilegia, anemones and bearded irises make way for the first roses and eager perennials. Greening crowns of thalictrum, echinacea and rudbeckia stretch to fill the gaps as I continue to cross my fingers for at least one peony from my temperamental lot.

**Previous page:** A large autumn arrangement of leaves and seed heads from my garden.
**Above:** 'Mum's Spring Garden' (page 58) on my dressing table.

# My favourite spring pickings

AQUILEGIA BLOOMS AND FOLIAGE • DAFFODILS • TULIPS • RANUNCULUS • SWEET PEA BLOOMS AND TENDRILS • BLOSSOM • SPRING BRANCHES • PEONIES • LUPINS • FENNEL • BEARDED IRISES • HEUCHERA • NIGELLA • NEMESIA • JASMINE • NARCISSI • LILY OF THE VALLEY • NASTURTIUM BLOOMS AND FOLIAGE • HONEYSUCKLE • PENSTEMON • PURPLE TOADFLAX • FORGET-ME-NOTS • ANEMONES • CORNFLOWERS • FOXGLOVES • FRITILLARIA • ALLIUMS • IXIA • WATTLE • PAPER DAISIES • SNOWFLAKES • WISTERIA • PUSSY WILLOW • PHLOMIS • ROSES • GEUMS

# EARLY CHEER

While daffodils sing spring, they also bring brightness to the tail end of winter. I love the acid yellow of these giant beauties, combined with the fragrant, soft cream swirls of the little narcissi, 'Erlicheer'. Spikes of wattle, paper daisies and self-seeded snow daisies sprinkle dots of yellow, all offset by the lipstick-pink tips of beautiful jasmine. These were easily gathered together without additional help in an antique ceramic jar found at the back of a second-hand store.

·

Remember, when using daffodils or any sappy stems, to pick and rest in water separately before arranging with other plants. Their stems need to seal to avoid poisoning the vase water and reducing the length of your arrangement's life.

CUMBERLAND
DAIRY Co Ld
PURE
THICK CREAM
FRESH DAILY
LOW ROW.
Nr CARLISLE

*I turned a blind eye to the old wives' tale that it is bad luck to bring wattle inside.*

# EARLY CHEER

Large yellow daffodil – *Narcissus* 'Carlton' / Creamy and fragrant smaller narcissus – *Narcissus* 'Erlicheer' / Common jasmine (which can be quite weedy!) – *Jasminum polyanthum* / White paper daisy – *Rhodanthe anthemoides* / Snow daisy – *Chrysanthemum paludosum* / Early green wattle – *Acacia decurrens*.

# SPRING SALAD

The acid greens of spring leaves can bring as much zest as the vibrancy of autumn colour. Here I gave my fruiting plums and a roadside apple tree a naughty spring haircut to capture the energy they bring. The old-fashioned plum trees, pictured here with both burgundy and green leaves, are the first to blossom in my garden but I equally love their young, immature fruit that follows. So glossy and firm, hanging in drops from their branches.

•

Apple blossom is by far my favourite of all blossoms and I am always gripped in anticipation of its arrival – a little later than the others. I don't think there is anything more romantic than the blush tips of apple blossom buds. The arrangement is built in a large second-hand soup bowl with chicken wire support and pot tape to secure.

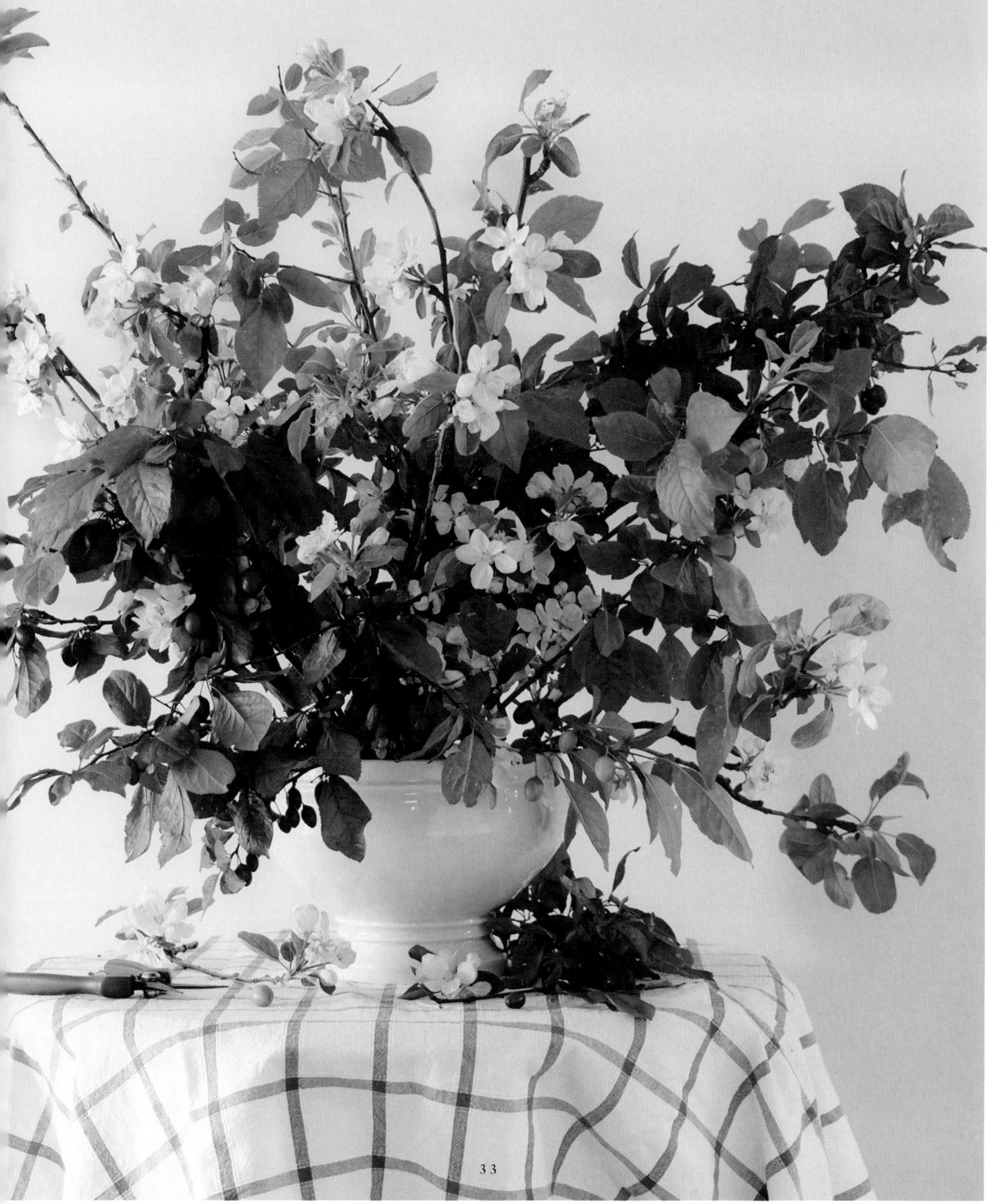

Apple blossom
(foraged)

Plum tree
with immature
plums

Greengage
plum

# SPRING SALAD
Roadside apple tree – *Malus domestica* / Purple leaf plum – *Prunus cerasifera* / Greengage plum – *Prunus domestica.*

# THE
# COTTAGE

With my attention captured by all the emerging little gems, I set
out to create a small garden scene. Channelling the loose idea of
a romantic 'crop' of a cottage garden, I used the lovely shapes of
aquilegia and thalictrum foliage with tendrils of sweet pea to map
the loose but low overall outline.

·

Using an old-fashioned trough-style ceramic vase I found online,
packed with a rectangular pillow of chicken wire, I gently poked
in the delicate heads of blue forget-me-nots, thyme, daisies,
chartreuse heads of fennel and a few bright highlights of red geum.
Creamy white and blush sweet peas filled spaces partnered with a
single blue cornflower.

·

This is a real example of making use of what I had. If just one
pickable stem is available, I'll take it and find it a home inside.

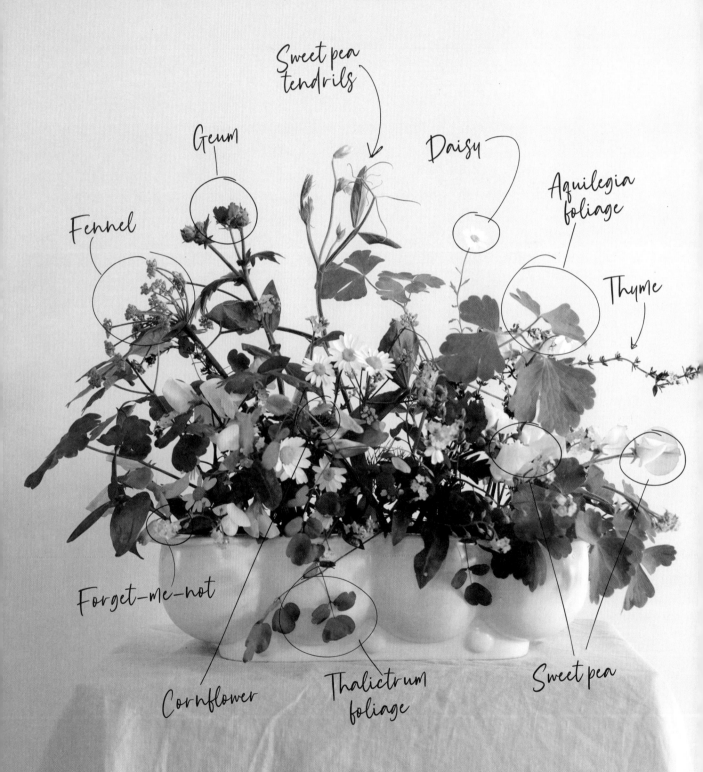

Sweet pea tendrils

Geum

Daisy

Aquilegia foliage

Fennel

Thyme

Forget-me-not

Sweet pea

Cornflower

Thalictrum foliage

*Never underestimate the whimsy that sweet pea tendrils bring to an arrangement.*

# THE COTTAGE

Sweet pea – *Lathyrus odoratus* 'High Scent' and *Lathyrus odoratus* 'Aoraki' / Fennel – *Foeniculum vulgare* / Snow daisy – *Chrysanthemum paludosum* / Red geum – *Geum chiloense* 'Mrs Bradshaw' / Self-seeded forget-me-not – *Myosotis scorpioides* / Common thyme – *Thymus vulgaris* / Blue cornflower – *Centaurea cyanus* / Self-seeded aquilegia (commonly known as granny's bonnet or columbine) – *Aquilegia vulgaris* / Thalictrum – *Thalictrum delavayi* 'Hewitt's Double'.

# SHOWGIRL

With a huge abundance of the fun sweet pea 'Blue Shift' in the garden, I decided to play further in the same palette. Opening as magenta, deepening to purple then fading to blue, I complemented the sweet peas with some frou-frou bearded irises, jewel-coloured aquilegia and rich green foliage from a neighbour's elder tree that was poking through the fence. Airy, cream heuchera flower and spiky purple toadflax fade out the top line and all were plunged into a tall, glam brass vase. The sweet peas were still flowering on lovely extra long stems, but due to their delicacy I added them last, poking them in to be supported on each other and the surrounding stems, with toes still reaching the water. I love the resulting luxurious overflow effect.

Purple
toadflax

Heuchera

Aquilegia

Spring
foliage of
elder

Sweet pea

Bearded
iris

Sweet pea
tendrils

# SHOWGIRL

Sweet pea – *Lathyrus odoratus* 'Blue Shift' / Self-seeded aquilegia (commonly known as granny's bonnet or columbine) – *Aquilegia vulgaris* / Purple bearded iris – *Iris x germanica* / Heuchera flowers of *Heuchera villosa* 'Autumn Bride' / Purple toadflax (commonly considered a weed) – *Linaria purpurea* / Green spring growth of elder tree – *Sambucus nigra.*

# GIN & TONIC

Not far from my house is an enormous tract of land that was formerly
residential neighbourhoods. Following the 2011 Christchurch earthquake,
all homes, structures and utilities were removed as it was deemed unsafe
for dwelling. While the decision-makers grapple with its best future use,
those in my area use it for recreation; walking themselves, children and
dogs through the trees and shrubs that remain. These remnants of curated
gardens could be considered ghostly and sad, however, I have enjoyed
gently foraging among them, educating myself on new plants and what is
seasonally available. I like to think this is a nod to those that once lived there.

·

This giant, tumbling arrangement conjures up lounging under a dreamy
wisteria-covered patio, refreshing drink in hand, surrounded by springtime.
Using a second-hand urn I found online and firmly filled with chicken wire, I
enjoyed the opportunity to create on a large scale due to using (sensitively)
collected tree branches. The acid spectrum of greens seen in the gleditsia,
euphorbia and snowball viburnum are offset perfectly by the trailing
streams of ombre wisteria.

·

When using sappy stems like euphorbia, cut them to desired length (avoid
getting any on your hands) and then hydrate separately to your other plants
before placing in the arrangement. The aim is to allow them to dispel as much
sap as possible then seal to prevent contamination of the vase water.

*All foraged

Gleditsia

Snowball viburnum

Euphorbia

Wisteria

# GIN & TONIC

Japanese wisteria – *Wisteria floribunda* / Euphorbia (otherwise known as Mediterranean spurge) – *Euphorbia characias* / Snowball viburnum – *Viburnum macrocephalum* / Gleditsia – *Gleditsia triacanthos var. inermis* 'Sunburst'.

# LOLLY SCRAMBLE

While my own peony-growing efforts have left a lot to be desired, spring deliveries from my peony farming cousins, The Peony People, bring such delight! Fresh off a forage where I collected some dotty pink lupins and lemon-coloured tree lupins, I did a rough pluck of trailing nasturtium from the garden then I opened my delivery of 'Sarah Bernhardt' peonies and got playing.

•

Using a wonky, trophy-style vase I had scooped up at a second-hand store, I concentrated on working with the stems' natural movement. The result is playful with a 'just picked' vibe and the colour palette feels fresh and pretty.

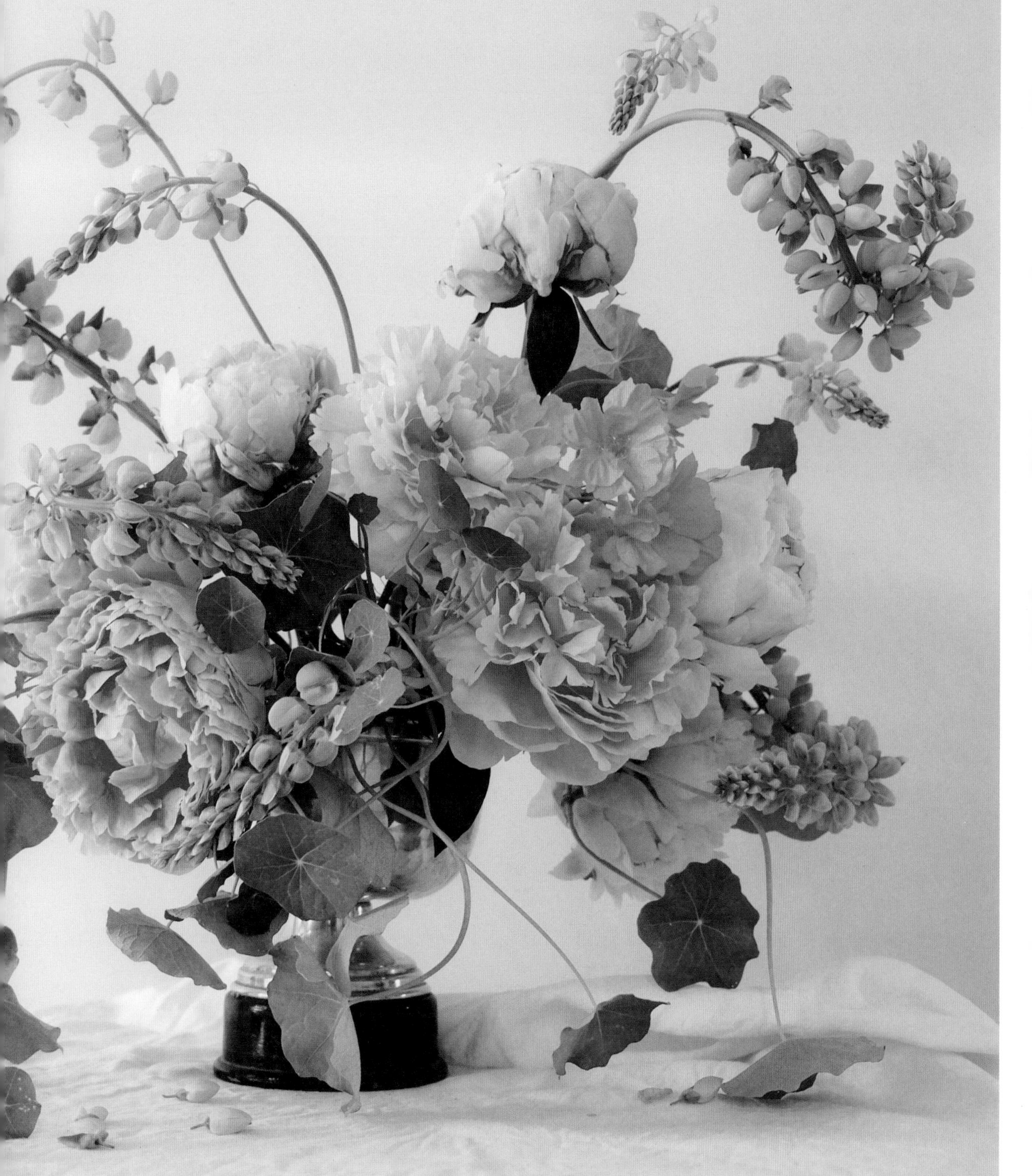

Tree lupin (foraged)

Nasturtium flower

Lupin (foraged)

Peony

Nasturtium foliage

*Trailing foliage injects romance to any arrangement.*

# LOLLY SCRAMBLE

Foraged perennial pink lupin, variety unknown – *Lupinus* / Yellow tree lupin (commonly considered a weed) – *Lupinus arboreus* / Garden nasturtium – *Tropaeolum majus* / Peony – *Paeonia lactiflora* 'Sarah Bernhardt'.

# PETAL POWER

Bright, playful and pretty quirky, this arrangement is a version of the one that appeared on the cover of my first book *Petal Power*. For me it reflects the carefree fun that can be had when experimenting with flowers at your own kitchen bench. Never in pursuit of perfection, just gentle time working with your hands in silence.

•

Using a fabulous handmade vase by New Zealand ceramicist Wundaire, I filled it with chicken wire and proceeded to play around with the varying shapes, forms and colour. The chartreuse umbellifers of the fennel are wacky and provide fabulous support lower down for the dainty, lipstick-pink frills of nemesia. The bold red geums and single Iceland poppy contrast strongly with the pale aquilegia, marshmallow heads of peonies and those romantic bells of foxglove. Thalictrum foliage combined with the odd snapdragon and lovely stars of roadside buttercups complete the bold palette and happy vibe.

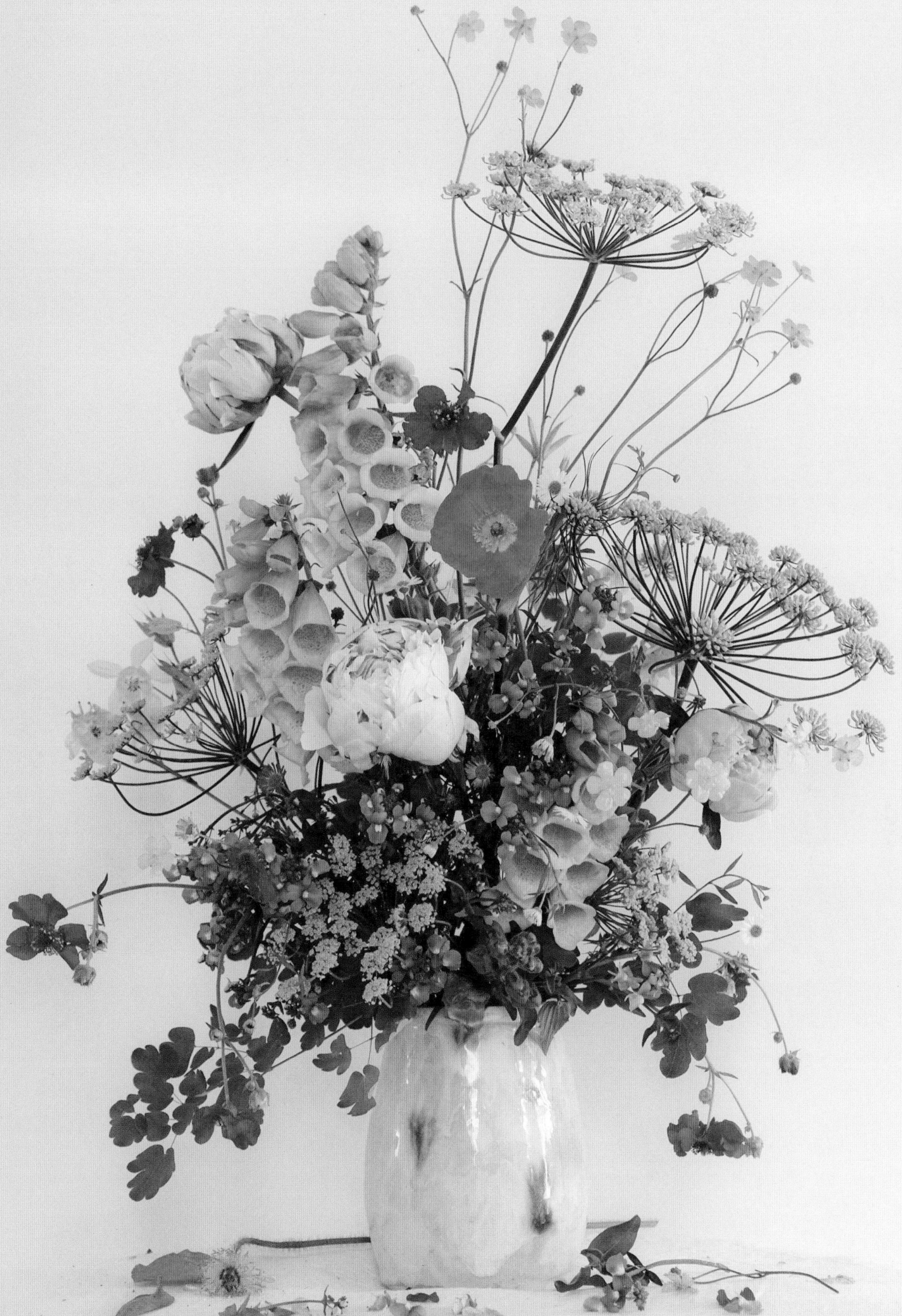

Buttercup (foraged)

Foxglove

Peony

Iceland poppy

Fennel

Aquilegia

Nemesia

Daisy

Geum

Snapdragon

Thalictrum foliage

Vase by Wundaire

*While tempting to pick earlier, avoid sulking fennel by picking when flowers are acid bright or in early stages of forming seed.*

# PETAL POWER

Foxglove – *Digitalis purpurea* 'Apricot' / Common fennel – *Foeniculum vulgare* / Red geum – *Geum chiloense* 'Mrs Bradshaw' / Self-seeded aquilegia (commonly known as granny's bonnet or columbine) – *Aquilegia vulgaris* / Snapdragon – *Antirrhinum majus* 'Madame Butterfly' / Pink nemesia – *Nemesia caerulea* / Mexican daisy – *Erigeron karvinskianus* / Iceland poppy – *Papaver nudicaule* / Tall buttercup – *Ranunculus acris* / Peony – *Paeonia lactiflora* 'Sarah Bernhardt' / Thalictrum – *Thalictrum delavayi* 'Hewitt's Double'.

# INTO THE WILD

Ultimately, it's hard to beat the common foxglove for its whimsical, fairy tale vibes. Ombre bells sliding from lipstick-pink to white are made even better by their freckles and twisting stems. Taking into account their poisonous attributes, I carefully harvested these from bush-bordered tracks behind our family holiday house in the Marlborough Sounds. Without the regular arranging kit I have at home, I got creative with an old preserving pot, laying a bundle of prostrate kōwhai inside then roughly weaving wisteria prunings around the edges and across the top to secure. This haphazard, natural support system worked extremely well and allowed me to make a huge arrangement with my foxglove finds.

Due to their toxicity, when handling all parts of the plant, be sure to thoroughly wash hands afterwards and place out of reach of children when unattended.

I used a ball of kōwhai in the base of a large preserving pot and wove a grid of wisteria prunings over the top for extra support.

Common foxglove – *Digitalis purpurea*.

# MUM'S SPRING GARDEN

As a farmer, my mother has always had more space to garden than she may have wanted. Her dislike of working in the garden is only balanced by her love of flowers. It's not that she doesn't thrive in her time spent in nature, it's that she has so many other physical activities in the outdoors that she enjoys more! Nonetheless, there has and will always be terrific variety to be found in the beds that she curates, and this collection reflects her style perfectly.

·

I love the nostalgia in the old-fashioned roses, along with the love-in-a-mist (nigella) that she always has a raging, self-seeded crop of. The fantastical long-spurred aquilegia is offset by balls of pink armeria and arms of weeping pear. It's those giant 'egg-like' peonies that captivate me the most with their creamy petals and fuzzy orange centres. Romantic, nostalgic and ramshackle in a ceramic urn, supported internally by chicken wire.

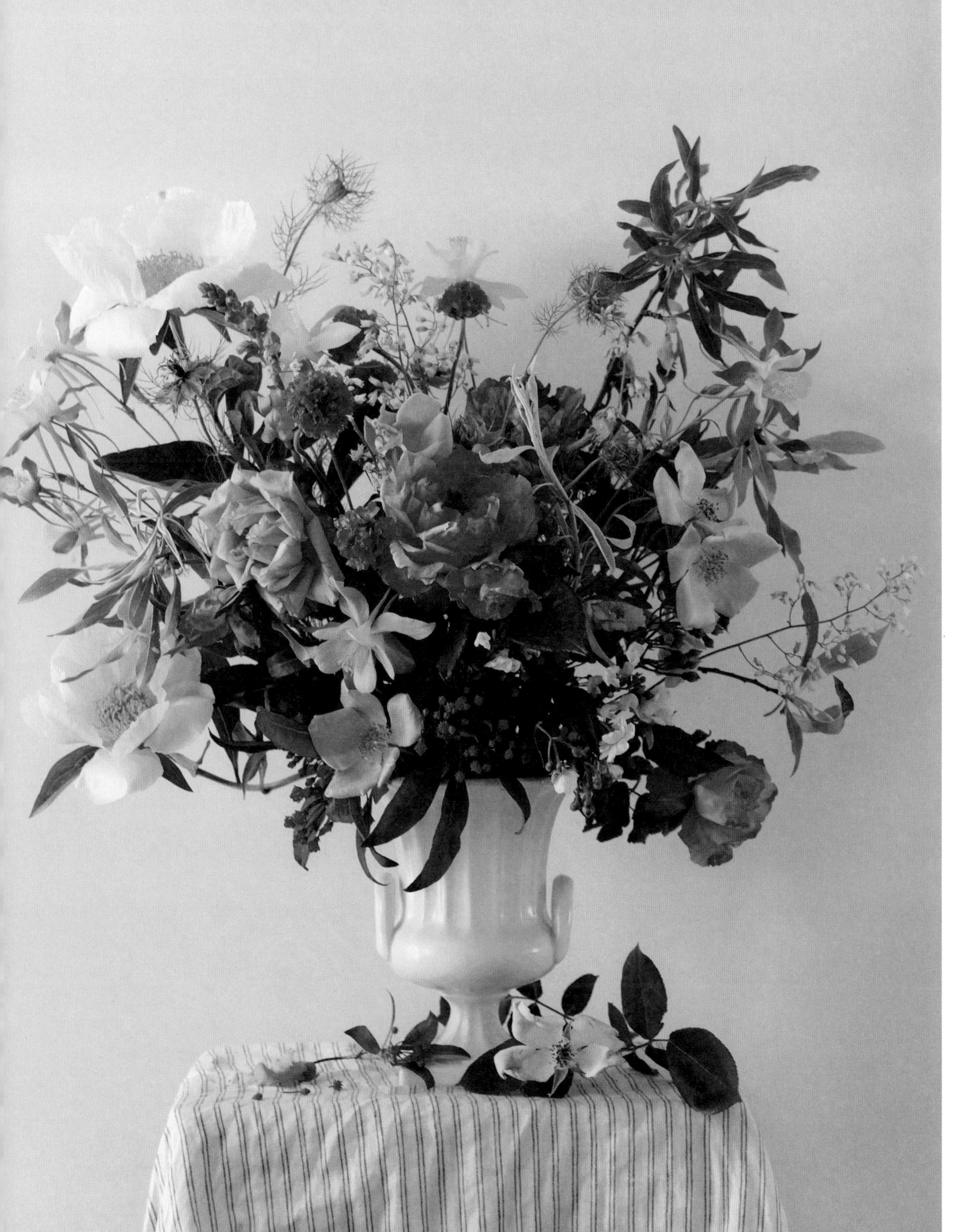

Snapdragon

Weeping pear

Heuchera

Nigella

Armeria

Aquilegia

Rose

Peony

Salvia

Kalmia

Rose

# MUM'S SPRING GARDEN

White peony – *Paeonia lactiflora* 'White wings' / Weeping pear – *Pyrus salicifolia* / Long-spurred aquilegia (commonly known as granny's bonnet or columbine) – *Aquilegia vulgaris* / Nigella (commonly known as love-in-a-mist) – *Nigella sativa* / Armeria (commonly known as thrift) – *Armeria maritima* 'Pacific Giant' / Pink kalmia – *Kalmia latifolia* 'Pink Charm' / White salvia – *Salvia hybrid* 'Glare' / Snapdragon – *Antirrhinum majus* / Green-leaved heuchera – *Heuchera* / Open-petaled, pink with soft yellow centre rose – *Rosa* 'The Alexandra Rose' / Large old-fashioned rose – *Rosa* 'General Gallieni'.

# MRS HOLMES & NEIGHBOURS

In late November I joined my sister and nieces for an elderflower foraging mission in the wilder depths of the Ōtākaro Avon River Corridor in Christchurch (following the 2011 earthquake, the area was deemed unstable for buildings so all houses were removed, with only the trees and shrubs of the properties remaining). My focus was quickly lost when we followed an overgrown path to a hidden area that had clearly been a loved garden.

·

An enormous rambling 'Sally Holmes' rose was perched at the river's edge while small climbing roses tumbled down from unkempt trees. I decided to collect everything I could find from this one area in honour of both what was lost, but also the plants that had continued to thrive. Long tendrils of honeysuckle and curling lupins were then combined with weedier, wild friends like vetch, cat's ear, tree lupins and forget-me-nots. All were hauled home and gathered together in the silver champagne bucket from our wedding day, filled generously with chicken wire and secured with pot tape.

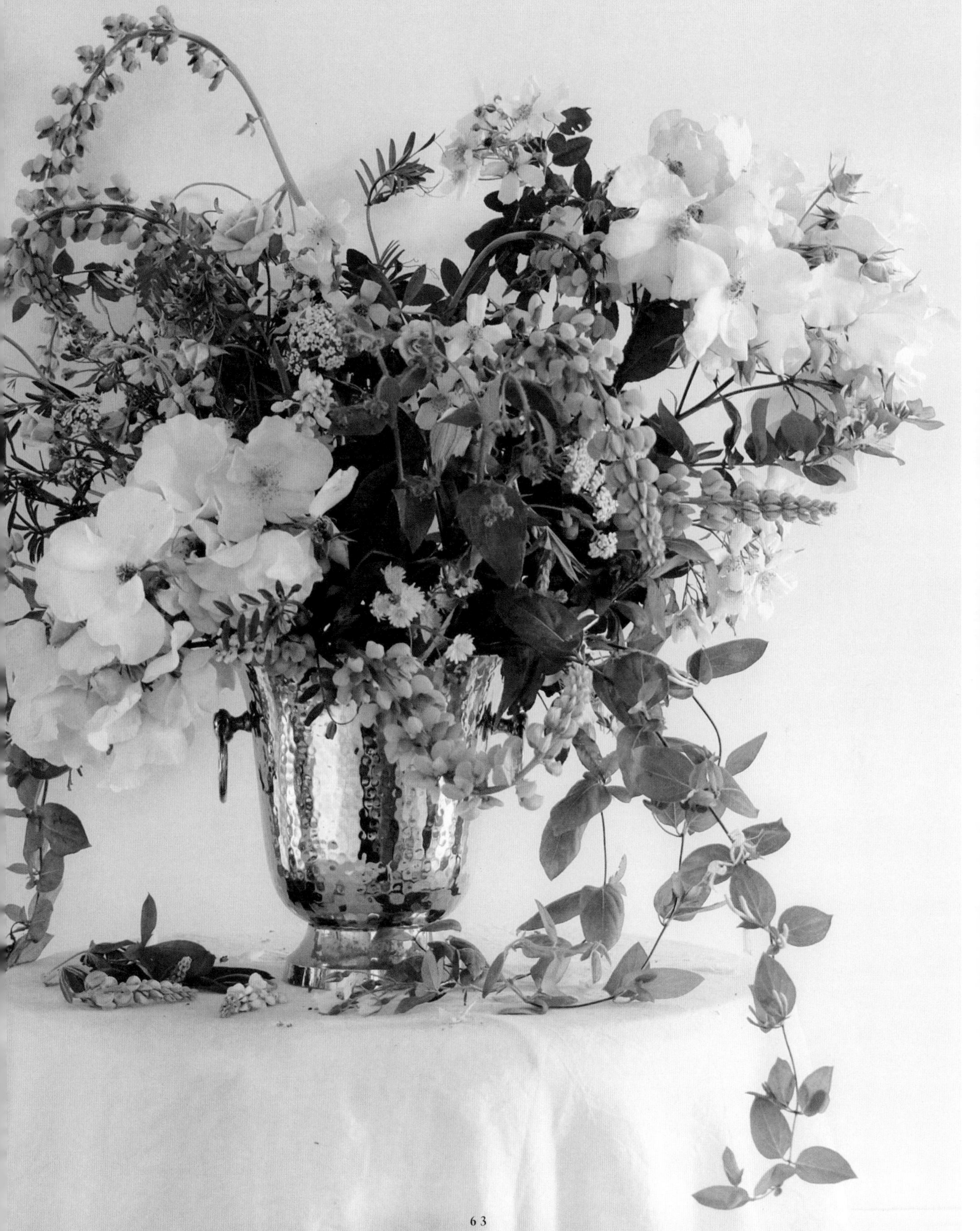

*I begin with my most plentiful stems which are wisteria and tree lupin...*

*...I make sure to position the wavy lupin to bend outward, away from the centre of the arrangement...*

*...I test to see where the stems work best in relation to their natural bends...*

*...I position the large rose stems on a diagonal to each other for visual balance...*

*...the smallest, daintiest stems and blooms are threaded in last, ensuring they reach the vase water.*

*All foraged

Forget-me-not

Lupin

Vetch

Rose

Rose

Tree lupin

Yarrow

Cat's ear

Honeysuckle

*It's easy for dainty blooms to get lost, but they do provide dimension and intrigue to a large arrangement.*

# MRS HOLMES & NEIGHBOURS

Large soft pink and white rose – *Rosa* 'Sally Holmes' / Pink miniature rose – *Rosa unknown* / White climbing rose – *Rosa unknown* / Foraged perennial pink lupin, variety unknown – *Lupinus* / Yellow tree lupin (commonly considered a weed) – *Lupinus arboreus* / Japanese honeysuckle – *Lonicera japonica* / Self-seeded forget-me-not – *Myosotis scorpioides* / Cat's ear (commonly mistaken for its dandelion cousin) – *Hypochaeris radicata* / Vetch – *Vicia sativa* / Common yarrow (cultivated varieties are often called achillea) – *Achillea millefolium*.

# BLUE MOON

A sweet little arrangement championing the first of my 'Blue Moon' rose blooms for the year. Somehow, I had managed to grow it in a wine barrel where it happily thrived all season! Deliciously interesting in its lilac tones, I had a quick scavenge to find other romantic friends for a small arrangement to pop in the bathroom. In an antique vase I bought online, I added tendrils of honeysuckle, spikes of purple toadflax, creamy sweet peas, a sprig of *Verbena bonariensis* and soft white and green foxgloves. This feels unfussy but sumptuous.

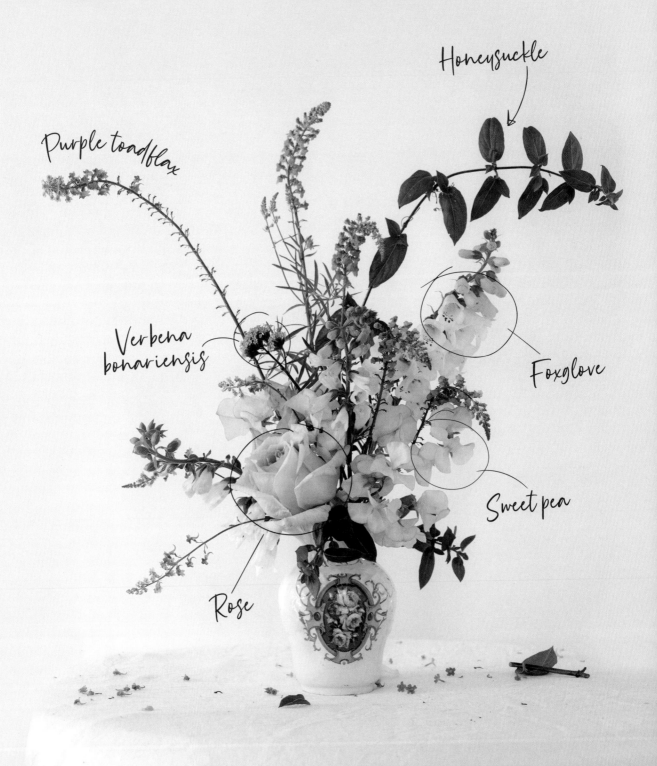

Honeysuckle

Purple toadflax

Verbena bonariensis

Foxglove

Sweet pea

Rose

*Verbena bonariensis is a long-time favourite. It adds such airy beauty to garden beds, but be warned, it's a very enthusiastic self-seeder!*

# BLUE MOON

Lilac-coloured rose – *Rosa* 'Blue Moon' / Japanese honeysuckle – *Lonicera japonica* / Purple toadflax (commonly considered a weed) – *Linaria purpurea* / Sweet pea – *Lathyrus odoratus* 'High Scent' / White speckled foxglove – *Digitalis purpurea* / Purple top vervain – *Verbena bonariensis*.

# SUMMER

For me, summer is about warm winds, breezy dresses, bean bags under the cherry tree and watering walks in the gloaming. Hot-weather watering is central to my little gardening life and there has never been a better connector to the season. Barefoot with the hose dragging behind, alarms set for irrigation systems and enforced time to tend and visit with all my garden creatures. I truly look forward to it.

Summer also signals the arrival of the louder residents of my garden. Cartoonish echinacea and rudbeckia weave through ethereal knautia, scabiosa, *Verbena bonariensis* and sanguisorba. Thalictrum finally releases its clouds of soft pink and white bells, while astrantia begins to arrive shining its stars from the darker depths of the beds. There is both never enough and too much to pick from, resulting in vibrant, rambling arrangements that make me smile with their quirkiness. Strawberries are sacrificed to drape over the edges of vases and I feel no shame in my bolting parsley, knowing how brilliantly it picks.

Previous page: Branches of gleditsia, snowball viburnum and apple blossom on the mantelpiece in my studio. Original paintings by UK-based New Zealand artist Stacey Gledhill. **Above:** 'The Joy Farmer' arrangement (page 106) set up for art inspiration.

## My favourite summer pickings

ROSES • DELPHINIUMS • LARKSPUR • COSMOS • RUDBECKIA • HELENIUMS • ECHINACEA • SCABIOSA • KNAUTIA MACEDONICA • DAHLIAS • JAPANESE ANEMONES • VERBENA BONARIENSIS • VERBENA RIGIDA • SANGUISORBA OFFICINALIS • ASTILBE • THALICTRUM • ASTRANTIA • SNAPDRAGONS • SHASTA DAISIES • ORLAYA • GEUMS • MARJORAM • STRAWBERRIES • PARSLEY • PANSIES • NEMESIA • CARNATIONS • VERONICA • POPPIES • AMMI MAJUS • STOCK • NIGELLA • FENNEL • BOG SAGE • CLEMATIS • MEXICAN DAISIES • ALCHEMILLA MOLLIS • ZINNIAS

# SHRINE TO DELPHI

A pretty wacky arrangement dictated in full by the glorious giant delphinium that toppled during a gusty day. I positioned it as a central tower in an urn, propped up in a cage of chicken wire, then scavenged around the garden for its audience. Twisty spires of purple toadflax fan around the central bloom with a little 'garden' of creamy penstemon, cornflowers, daisies, lobelia, pansies and strawberries gathering around the base. It became a kind of weather-triggered shrine!

•

It's really easy to overlook the smaller, delicate blooms in the garden, but use strong, surrounding stems to prop them up, always making sure their stems reach the vase water.

Delphinium

Purple toadflax

Pansy

Penstemon

Astilbe

Strawberry foliage

Cornflower

Lobelia

Daisy

Strawberry

# SHRINE TO DELPHI

Pacific giant delphinium – *Delphinium elatum* / Purple toadflax (commonly considered a weed) – *Linaria purpurea* / Beardtongue white penstemon – *Penstemon* 'Snowstorm' / Blue cornflower – *Centaurea cyanus* / Blue lobelia – *Lobelia erinus* 'Crystal Palace' / Mexican daisy – *Erigeron karvinskianus* / Cream astilbe – *Astilbe arendsii* 'Diamant' / Pansy – *Viola x wittrockiana* 'Delta Lavender Rose' Mix / Garden strawberry – *Fragaria x ananassa.*

# LATE LUNCH

Romantic, loose and low lying, this type of arrangement would
be very happy merging in with a cheeseboard, bread and wine!
While most people will sigh in frustration, bolting parsley means
great green flowers that can sub in as supporting foliage in a
vase. I used these to map out a gentle undulating top line, then
backfilled with penstemon, thalictrum, veronica and sweet peas.
With supportive chicken wire in the base, I played with scale by
adding three blousy roses, throwing some whimsy into the mix
with such contrasting scale.

Penstemon

Thalictrum

Parsley flower

Scabiosa

Sweet pea seed pod

Veronica

Sweet pea

Parsley foliage

Rose

Hydrangea

# LATE LUNCH

Lilac-coloured rose – *Rosa* 'Blue Moon' / Garden parsley – *Petroselinum crispum* / White scabiosa – *Scabiosa caucasica* 'Fama White' / Thalictrum with pink bell-shaped flowers (commonly known as Meadow Rue) – *Thalictrum delavayi* / Beardtongue white penstemon – *Penstemon* 'Snowstorm' / White lacecap hydrangea – *Hydrangea macrophylla var. normalis* / White veronica – *Veronica longifolia* 'Alba' / Sweet pea – *Lathyrus odoratus* 'High Scent'.

# SPICE GIRLS

When we first moved into our villa, the removal of these wall-hung spice shelves were high on my hit list. However, being a 'stuff' person, they quickly attracted little possessions and provided an unexpected opportunity for a revolving, seasonal still life.

Away from destructive cat paws, they have been the ideal spot to pop stems at loose ends, towering limbs of fennel, budded-up branches to force into flower, gone-to-seed herbs and long-lasting blooms that have outlived all their other friends from the vase. Looking back through my photos, this spot in my kitchen has become a visual diary of the seasons, my garden and surrounds.

Spring

Summer

**Spring from left:** Messy bottle of *Verbena bonariensis*, *Verbena rigida*, the odd nigella, common forget-me-not and blue cornflowers. These are joined by a single delphinium and stem of phlomis. The little silver vase contains a twisted jumble of red geums. **Summer from left:** Gone-to-seed spinach, coriander and sweet pea vines. **Autumn from left:** Fennel and marjoram. **Winter from left:** Japanese anemone seed heads, dried sedum, dried sanguisorba, echinacea and poppy heads.

# TINY DANCER

After hearing some sad news from a close friend, I nipped into the garden for a breather, returning with this mixed bunch of odd finds. Making use of a new vase from New Zealand-based maker Martha Blanche Sidonie, some chicken wire and my besty's favourite song 'Tiny Dancer' by Elton John, I started to play. This is certainly a balance of bold and soft lines with the strong graphic shape of the spring onion offset by the ethereal bells of thalictrum and frothiness of the roses. I placed the taller stems slightly off-centre and balanced the height by letting the winding arms of sweet pea tendrils play out to the side.

Spring onion

Thalictrum

Sweet pea

Daisy

Rose

Clematis

Daisy

Sweet pea tendrils

Vase by Martha Blanche Sidonie

*Don't overlook your vege garden for fun vase candidates!*

# TINY DANCER

Spring onion – *Allium chinense* / Thalictrum with pink bell-shaped flowers (commonly known as Meadow Rue) - *Thalictrum delavayi* / White rose – *Rosa* 'Iceberg' / Sweet pea – *Lathyrus odoratus* 'High Scent' / Old man's beard (noxious weed creeping through my neighbour's fence!) - *Clematis vitalba* / Snow daisy – *Chrysanthemum paludosum* / Shasta daisy – *Leucanthemum* 'Paladin'.

# HAPPY NEW YEAR

This arrangement features 'everyone' from my garden in January and is my best go at creating festive, floral fireworks! I was interested to see what the result would be when challenged to use every bloom I could gather. Paying little attention to offering up key focal points, I did away with foliage and used flowers only. One person's headache is another's heaven!

•

As with so many of my arrangements, this one was built knowing it would have its back to the wall, viewed only from the front in its position on the mantelpiece. I used my longest and strongest stems first including fennel, sanguisorba, the sunflower and rudbeckia to map out a loose, fanned outline. As I began to backfill, the stronger stems of echinacea took priority as they would be handy to support top-heavy plants like cosmos, helenium and scabiosa between them. Like most garden-sourced flowers, I didn't have the luxury of choosing an easy balance of flower types, instead just offering every specimen a spot within the loud crowd.

•

The arrangement is supported perfectly in the ceramic urn, tightly packed with chicken wire.

Echinacea

Sanguisorba

Astilbe

Sunflower

Geum

Fennel

Verbena
rigida

Rudbeckia

Orlaya

Japanese
anemone

Helenium

Knautia

Echinacea

Snapdragon

Daisy

Thalictrum

Scabiosa

Cosmos

*Echinacea pallida 'Hula Dancer' is a particular favourite with its long, droopy petals.*

# HAPPY NEW YEAR

Large yellow rudbeckia (commonly known as black-eyed Susan or coneflower) – *Rudbeckia hirta* 'Irish Eyes' / Pink-petaled echinacea (commonly known as coneflower) are different cultivars of *Echinacea purpurea* / White echinacea – *Echinacea purpurea* 'Alba' / Pale pink echinacea with very long petals – *Echinacea pallida* 'Hula Dancer' / Common fennel – *Foeniculum vulgare* / Sanguisorba (commonly known as greater burnet) – *Sanguisorba officinalis* / Tall-growing pink thalictrum – *Thalictrum delavayi* 'Hewitt's Double' / Pink astilbe – *Astilbe chinensis var. taquetii* 'Lilac' / Pink Japanese anemone – *Anemone x hybrida* 'Richard Ahrens' / Burgundy cosmos – *Cosmos bipinnatus* 'Rubenza' / Snapdragon – *Antirrhinum majus* 'Madame Butterfly' / Knautia (commonly known as scabious) – *Knautia macedonica* 'Red Cherries' / Dark scabiosa – *Scabiosa atropurpurea* 'Black Knight' / Red geum – *Geum chiloense* 'Mrs Bradshaw' / Slender vervain – *Verbena rigida* / Orlaya (commonly known as white lace flower) – *Orlaya grandiflora* / Helenium (commonly known as sneezeweed) – *Helenium* 'Waltraut' / Sunflower – *Helianthus annuus* 'White' / Shasta daisy – *Leucanthemum x superbum* 'Fluffy'.

# PARTY ANIMALS

The real advantage of growing a wide variety of graphic, interesting blooms is that just a few rough handfuls can inject a huge amount of personality to your inside spaces. Bright bobble heads, spindly umbellifers and vivid petals provide a casual but vibrant vibe for a party!

Using simple, old glass bottles, I popped pickings of heleniums, cosmos and bog sage in each, varying stem lengths to work with the height of the vessels. The airy nature of the flowers makes them ideal candidates for dotting down a table or scattering through a room.

Making the most of my scopey garden plants like fennel, *Verbena bonariensis*, rudbeckia and Japanese anemones, I completed the family of arrangements with a large one that would happily hold court from a sideboard or even the floor. All were created quickly and with less regard than usual to placement, instead letting the colours and shapes mingle easily for a casual effect.

**Plants featured in small arrangements:** Bog sage – *Salvia uliginosa* / Burgundy cosmos – *Cosmos bipinnatus* 'Rubenza' / Helenium (commonly known as sneezeweed) – *Helenium* 'Waltraut' / Small yellow rudbeckia (commonly known as black-eyed Susan or coneflower) – *Rudbeckia* 'Goldsturm'.
**Plants featured in tall arrangement:** Large yellow rudbeckia (commonly known as black-eyed Susan or coneflower) – *Rudbeckia hirta* 'Irish Eyes' / White Japanese anemone – *Anemone x hybrida* 'White Knight' / Pink Japanese anemone – *Anemone x hybrida* 'Richard Ahrens' / Common fennel – *Foeniculum vulgare* / Purple top vervain – *Verbena bonariensis*.

# STRAWBERRIES & CREAM

Whenever I use this goblet-style vase, it feels like the results always resemble some kind of divine pudding! All the tasty sweet colours were out in the garden so I cruised around collecting the yummy tones and scoopable, decorative shapes in pinks, crimsons, greens and red. It's easy for me to imagine what would be crunchy, velvety, soft and crispy to nibble.

·

Using a smallish flower frog under an open cage of chicken wire, I worked from the edges up, leaving stems long where I could to achieve a balanced height.

Echinacea

Geum

Dahlia

Cosmos

Echinacea

Astilbe

Japanese anemone

Sanguisorba

Knautia

Marjoram

Snapdragon

Strawberry

Rose

Pansy

Thalictrum

Scabiosa

Nemesia

*The unusual colouring of Echinacea purpurea 'Giant Lime' looks as wonderful in the garden as it does in a mixed arrangement.*

# STRAWBERRIES & CREAM

Lilac-coloured rose – *Rosa* 'Blue Moon' / Decorative dahlia – *Dahlia* 'Flashback' / Pink-petaled echinacea (commonly known as coneflower) – *Echinacea purpurea* / Green-petaled echinacea – *Echinacea purpurea* 'Giant Lime' / Burgundy cosmos – *Cosmos bipinnatus* 'Rubenza' / Sanguisorba (commonly known as greater burnet) – *Sanguisorba officinalis* / Red geum – *Geum chiloense* 'Mrs Bradshaw' / Marjoram – *Origanum majorana* / Dark scabiosa – *Scabiosa atropurpurea* 'Black Knight' / Thalictrum with pink bell-shaped flowers – *Thalictrum delavayi* / Pink Japanese anemone – *Anemone x hybrida* 'Richard Ahrens' / Pink nemesia – *Nemesia caerulea* / Pink astilbe – *Astilbe chinensis var. taquetii* 'Lilac' / Snapdragon – *Antirrhinum majus* 'Madame Butterfly' / Pansy – *Viola x wittrockiana* 'Delta Lavender Rose' Mix / Garden strawberry – *Fragaria x ananassa* / Knautia (commonly known as scabious) – *Knautia macedonica* 'Red Cherries'.

# FROM AROUND THE EDGES

My discovery of gardening didn't stop at the gate. I entirely surprised myself when I started to be able to identify plants out in the 'real world'; it grew into a personal challenge that endlessly flipped through my head. Where I had never paid any attention to the rambling wild sweet peas that crept around the edges of dry Canterbury roadsides or wondered about the difference between dandelions and their cousins, I became consumed in both noticing and knowing.

•

This huge arrangement was gathered while biking forgotten little corners of my neighbourhood.

•

All of these plants are introduced species to New Zealand, that have simply taken off in glee in our climate and conditions. Plants like purple loosestrife are problematic around our waterways while others, like chicory and red clover, have escaped their primary uses in agriculture and taken for the wilds. They are called weeds which ultimately means they are 'plants growing in the wrong place'. It's very important to forage weeds responsibly, avoiding carrying any ripe seed heads away with you and spreading them unnecessarily.

*Using my most plentiful stems, I map out the loose outline...*

*...the structural loosestrife helps me achieve an asymmetrical balance...*

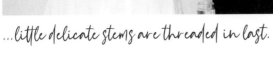

*...little delicate stems are threaded in last.*

Loosestrife

Buddleia

Tree lupin

Cat's ear

Chicory

Mallow

Red clover

Dock

Buchan weed

Yarrow

Viper's bugloss

Stinking mayweed

Broad-leaved sweet pea

# FROM AROUND THE EDGES

Viper's bugloss (often mistaken for blue borage) – *Echium vulgare* / Cat's ear (commonly mistaken for its dandelion cousin) – *Hypochaeris radicata* / Stinking mayweed (commonly mistaken for oxeye daisy) – *Anthemis cotula* / Chicory – *Cichorium intybus* / Buddleia (commonly called butterfly bush) – *Buddleja davidii* / Common white and pink yarrow (cultivated varieties are often called achillea) – *Achillea millefolium* / Mallow – *Malva sylvestris* / Perennial, broad-leaved sweet pea – *Lathyrus latifolius* / Tree lupin – *Lupinus arboreus* / Dock – *Rumex obtusifolius* / Red clover – *Trifolium pratense* / Buchan weed – *Hirschfeldia incana* / Purple loosestrife – *Lythrum salicaria.*

# THE JOY FARMER

For all the disruption, chaos and uncertainty caused by the
COVID-19 global pandemic, the forced pause during nationwide
lockdowns presented some silver linings. For me, it was what
spurred the writing of my first book; for my cousin Sarah
Rutherford, it triggered a step into the unknown with the planting
out of her first commercial cut-flower crop. The disruptions of
shipping and a greater awareness of 'where' our flowers are coming
from has timed in extremely well for the surge in small-scale,
outdoor-focused flower farms across the country. I have relished
watching Sarah and her business The Joy Farmer find its stride,
gaining knowledge from her own learnings and best of all, getting
to play with the results!

·

This giant, joyous collection in a large soup terrine, packed with
chicken wire and secured with pot tape, reflects the romantic,
garden-grown vibe that in my mind speaks of my dear cousin's
personal style as much as anything.

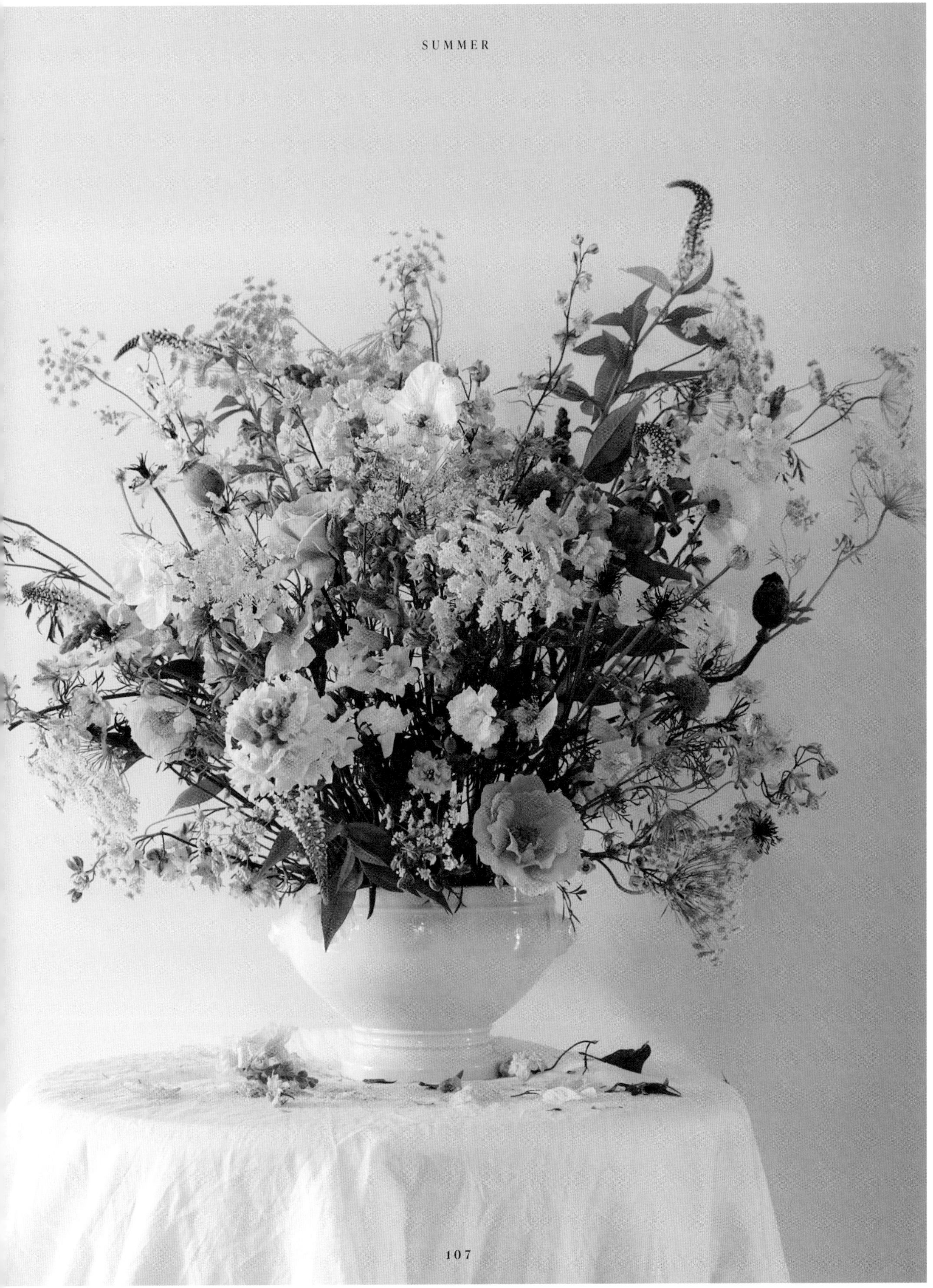

Iceland
poppy

Scabiosa
seed head

Gooseneck
loosestrife

Nigella

Poppy
seed head

Ammi
majus

Larkspur

Nigella

Snapdragon

Rose

Carnation

# THE JOY FARMER

Ammi (commonly known as Bishop's flower or False Queen Anne's lace) – *Ammi majus* / Larkspur – *Delphinium consolida* 'Smokey Eyes' / White nigella with black centre – *Nigella hispanica* 'African Bride' / Blue nigella with black centre – *Nigella papillosa* 'Spanish Midnight' / Carnation – *Dianthus caryophyllus* 'Enfant de Nice' Mix / Snapdragon – *Antirrhinum majus* 'Madame Butterfly' / Gooseneck loosestrife – *Lysimachia clethroides* / Poppy seed heads – *Papaver paeoniflorum* 'Poppy Peony Black' / Scabiosa seed heads – *Scabiosa stellata* 'Starball' / Iceland poppy – *Papaver nudicaule* 'Champagne Bubbles' Mix / Hybrid tea rose – *Rosa* 'Spiced Coffee'.

# SILVER LININGS

This is one of my favourite colour palettes I've pulled together.
In fact, I can imagine a sprawling tapestry of a garden bed using
these plants only. I love the rust of the sanguisorba versus the
bog sage blue and chartreuse of the fennel, musty green of the
poppy seed heads and flash of orange stamens. The colour and
the airy, unusual forms give the arrangement a lacy, wild vibe
which feels casual and summery.

•

Using an old pewter jug pilfered from my mum's cupboard, I was
able to create a loose, fan-shaped outline, using the fennel as
a guide and a filler for which the other softer-stemmed plants
could find support within.

*I use the structural, tall stems of fennel to map out an outline and find my scale for the jug…*

*...a simple, graphic dahlia with short stem finds its home as a statement...*

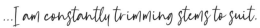

*...I am constantly trimming stems to suit.*

Veronica

Japanese
anemone

Echinacea

Poppy
seed heads

Fennel

Sanguisorba

Dahlia

Nigella

Bog sage

Echinacea

Dahlia

*I love nigella as much in bloom as I do its sculptural seed pod.*

# SILVER LININGS

Common fennel – *Foeniculum vulgare* / Sanguisorba (commonly known as greater burnet) – *Sanguisorba officinalis* / Bog sage – *Salvia uliginosa* / Nigella (commonly known as love-in-a-mist) – *Nigella sativa* / White veronica – *Veronica longifolia* 'Alba' / Poppy seed heads (commonly known as breadseed poppy) – *Papaver somniferum* / White Japanese anemone – *Anemone x hybrida* 'White Knight' / White echinacea – *Echinacea purpurea* 'Alba' / White self-seeded single-petal dahlia – *unknown* / White decorative dahlia – *Dahlia* 'White Aster'.

# AUTUMN

Every year, autumn always surprises me with the abundance still available for a vase. I seem to get seasonal amnesia, panicking as the days grow shorter and the air chillier, yet on looking closer, I find the cosmos and heleniums marching forward. Zinnias come into their own and I gratefully revel in the astonishing beauty of gifted chrysanthemums. Astrantia seems to get a turbo charge, glowing from the shady corners, buoying me along with the structural heads of sedum and my favourite, naked bobbles of Japanese anemone seed heads.

Without a doubt, the autumn light can be rivalled by no other season. As it tests the garden with cooler evenings, the sun starts to track lower, sprinkling the beds in fairy dust. Of all the seasons, it feels like autumn isn't trying to steal from the season before, instead, easing us into the shock of winter.

**Previous page:** Late summer in the garden. **Above:** 'The Great Gilroys' (page 132) on the mantelpiece in my office with collected treasures. Artwork on the left by me; artwork on the right by Maddy Young.

## My favourite autumn pickings

HOLLYHOCKS • CHRYSANTHEMUMS • DAHLIAS • ASTRANTIA • JAPANESE ANEMONE BLOOMS AND SEED HEADS • COSMOS • ZINNIAS • ROSES • SEDUM • ERYNGIUM • ROSEMARY • HYDRANGEAS • AUTUMN FOLIAGE • RASPBERRIES • SCABIOSA • HOPS • MONARDA • MINT • HONEYSUCKLE • SEED HEADS • ASTERS • DELPHINIUMS • AQUILEGIA FOLIAGE • HEBES • ROSEHIPS • CRAB APPLES • CHESTNUTS • VERBENA BONARIENSIS • VERBENA RIGIDA • HELENIUMS • FEVERFEW • PENSTEMON • NASTURTIUM • LUPINS • BOG SAGE • NEMESIA • ECHINACEA • RUDBECKIA

# SEASON OF THE SOUL

This big gathering of autumn treasures has that welcoming 'just picked' feeling. Using a large bulbous vase with a narrower opening, I attempted to keep stem lengths as long as possible to achieve a comfortable scale. The wonky, airy forms of Japanese anemones, their buds and structural parsley flowers offset the more graphic forms of the cosmos and hollyhocks. I find hollyhocks always look so messy in my garden, but give a fairy tale, old-fashioned vibe when included in arrangements. Nipping off spent flowers as they fade will give way for existing buds to bloom.

•

With some extra stems on hand, I played with adding some heat with bronze sunflowers and heleniums in contrast to a cooler version using blue bog sage. It's fun to experiment with colour palettes and tones to change the personality of what you create.

Parsley flower

Scabiosa

Japanese anemone

Hollyhock

Honeysuckle

Hollyhock

Japanese anemone

Cosmos

Raspberry

Cosmos

Clematis

*Warm it up by adding heleniums and sunflowers.*

*Cool it down by adding bog sage.*

# SEASON OF THE SOUL

Garden parsley – *Petroselinum crispum* / Unknown mix of peach, pink and white hollyhocks – *Alcea rosea* / Burgundy cosmos – *Cosmos bipinnatus* 'Rubenza' / Peach cosmos – *Cosmos bipinnatus* 'Apricot Lemonade' / White Japanese anemone – *Anemone x hybrida* 'White Knight' / Pink Japanese anemone – *Anemone x hybrida* 'Richard Ahrens' / Raspberry – *Rubus idaeus* 'Aspiring' / Old man's beard (noxious weed creeping through my neighbour's fence!) – *Clematis vitalba* / Japanese honeysuckle – *Lonicera japonica* / White scabiosa – *Scabiosa caucasica* 'Fama White' / Helenium (commonly known as sneezeweed) – *Helenium* 'Waltraut' / Sunflower – *Helianthus annuus* 'Bronze Shades' Mix / Bog sage – *Salvia uliginosa*.

# PINK LEMONADE

A goblet pudding of sorbet tones and fruity petals, this is an incredibly lush mix of what lingers in my garden in mid-autumn. One of my favourite flowers, astrantia, arrives from the shadowy parts of my garden where it brings such light and easily outlasts anything else in the vase. I very regularly re-snip its stems and use in another arrangement. Common garden herbs like marjoram and parsley are also terrific pickers and bring lovely supporting green to break up the sweetness and froth delivered by the snapdragons and dahlias. As always the pink and white Japanese anemones are so attractive in their floral form as well as their sweet round buds that almost look like insect antennae.

Cosmos

Parsley flower

Aster

Dahlia

Cosmos

Astrantia

Lupin

Marjoram

Japanese anemone

Feverfew

Nasturtium

Penstemon

Snapdragon

Dahlia

*Astrantia has incredible vase life! Don't be shy to graduate it from one dying arrangement into a new bunch.*

# PINK LEMONADE

White decorative dahlia – *Dahlia* 'White Aster' / Pink single-petal self-seeded dahlia – *unknown* / Pink decorative dahlia – *Dahlia* 'Flashback' / Burgundy cosmos – *Cosmos bipinnatus* 'Rubenza' / Peach cosmos – *Cosmos bipinnatus* 'Apricot Lemonade' / Marjoram – *Origanum majorana* / Garden parsley – *Petroselinum crispum* / White lupin – *Lupinus mutabilis var. cruckshankii* 'White Javelin' / White matricaria daisy (commonly known as feverfew) – *Tanacetum parthenium* / Garden nasturtium – *Tropaeolum majus* / White Japanese anemone – *Anemone x hybrida* 'White Knight' / Pink Japanese anemone – *Anemone x hybrida* 'Richard Ahrens' / Beardtongue white penstemon – *Penstemon* 'Snowstorm' / Aster (commonly known as a Michaelmas daisy) – *Symphyotrichum novi-belgii* / Snapdragon – *Antirrhinum majus* 'Madame Butterfly' / Astrantia (commonly known as masterwort) – *Astrantia major* 'Star Bush'.

*Begin with conditioning all stems, stripping away excess foliage.*

# FLOWERS FOR FRIENDS

The most surprising joy I have found in growing a flower garden is giving bunches of blooms to friends and family. Whipping around the garden with visitors then sending them home with a wee posy, its bottoms wrapped in a wet paper towel and contained in an old bread bag. Better yet is arming myself with a flowery gift for hosts, carefully contained with string-coated wire and housed in a water-filled, sawn-off plastic milk bottle squeezed into the car cupholder for transport. Whatever way the flowers arrive, there is no avoiding the grassroots, good nature of offering a home-grown posy.

Building an arrangement in a vase first or simply in your hands will do the trick. Sometimes it's fun to have a go at creating a circular bouquet as shown here.

*\*This bouquet was made using all the flowers from the previous 'Pink Lemonade' arrangement.*

Choosing one of your prettiest focal blooms, hold in your non-dominant hand and place the next

stem diagonally across the first. Grip gently with thumb and use other hand to give the stems a little turn.

Continue to add stems diagonally across the others, followed by a turn in the same direction. ⟶

Turning will gradually create a spiralling of the stems, effectively locking each stem in place to where

you intended it. This process has you forming your bouquet from centre outward. Once you have used

as many flowers as you choose, work around the posy adjusting placement and pulling blooms into view.

*"Whatever way the flowers
arrive, there is no avoiding the
grassroots, good nature of offering
a home-grown posy."*

Tie off with twine or string-coated wire then trim the bottom of the stems to the same length.

# THE GREAT GILROYS

Roses, the trophies of romance and femininity. As a relative newcomer to growing roses in my own garden, I took a field trip to learn more from local growers Gilroy Nurseries in North Canterbury. Walking the rainbow-coloured rows at dusk was like being in a fantastical movie set, and cemented my lust to learn more.

·

Armed with a bucket of beauty I came home and created an ode to my experience, highlighting the Gilroy-grown roses in all their sumptuous, luxurious forms. Aiming for an informal and theatrical vibe, I threaded them into a tall 'ice cream sundae' style vase that allowed me to build outward and with asymmetrical height.

The Alexandra Rose

Katherine Mansfield

Lady of Shalott

Rugosa scabrosa

Wollerton Old Hall

Roald Dahl

Ali Mau

*I will be forever besotted with the romance and storybook vibe of rosehips.*

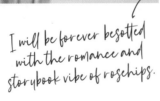

# THE GREAT GILROYS

*Rosa* 'Lady of Shalott' / *Rosa* 'Wollerton Old Hall' / *Rosa* 'Ali Mau' / *Rosa* 'Roald Dahl' / *Rosa* 'The Alexandra Rose' / *Rosa* 'Rugosa Scabrosa' / *Rosa* 'Katherine Mansfield'.

# PICK 'N' MIX

If you become really keen on arranging from your own garden, the key is to grow as much variety as you can. Even if you can't bring yourself to add really bold colour, consider curating an interesting mix of shapes and sizes of blooms, seed heads and foliage so the option of some whimsy is always at hand.

·

A quick autumn wander in my garden awarded me these weird and wonderful shapes from snipping only six different plants. Fuzzy, smooth, spiky, tufty, big, small, sweet and sour. All of these perennials are easy to grow and bring an interesting romance to a simple glass bottle.

Sea holly

Japanese
anemone
seed heads

Aster

Japanese
anemone

Verbena
bonariensis

Astrantia

# PICK 'N' MIX

Pink Japanese anemone – *Anemone x hybrida* 'Richard Ahrens' / Eryngium (commonly known as sea holly*)* – *Eryngium planum* 'Blue Hobbit' / Astrantia (commonly known as masterwort) – *Astrantia major* 'Star Bush' / Purple top vervain – *Verbena bonariensis* / Aster (commonly known as Michaelmas daisy) – *Aster salignus.*

# MUM'S AUTUMN GARDEN

By April, my own urban garden starts to feel like it is in major seasonal decline. Mum's garden beds, on the other hand, continue to offer up the goods. In the same spirit as the previously featured 'Mum's Spring Garden' (page 58), I sought to pick everything I could find, creating a visual snapshot of her curation.

•

I'm a bit obsessed with the moody colours of her fading hydrangeas when mixed with spiky rosemary and the saturated dahlias. Where young hydrangea blooms can be wilty and temperamental when picked, mature ones are glorious and halfway to being dried, needing no special treatment. The resulting 'pile' of flowers was supported by chicken wire, secured with pot tape in a large soup terrine.

Japanese anemone

Dahlia

Claret ash

Rose

Nigella

Rose

Hydrangea

Bog sage

Weeping pear

Sedum

Penstemon

Lupin

Rosemary

Dahlia

Hydrangea

Cosmos

Feverfew

*Sedum is not only a rewarding autumn bloom, but the sculptural heads can be dried for display.*

# MUM'S AUTUMN GARDEN

White and blue mophead hydrangeas fading to vintage tones – *Hydrangea macrophylla* / Large decorative dahlia – *unknown* / Single-petal peach dahlia – *unknown* / Self-seeded single-petal pink dahlia – *unknown* / White matricaria daisy (commonly known as feverfew) – *Tanacetum parthenium* 'White Stars' / Cosmos – *Cosmos bipinnatus* 'Cupcake' / Yellow rose – *Rosa* 'Friesia' / Pink-tinged rose – *Rosa* 'Strawberry Ice' / Weeping pear – *Pyrus salicifolia* / Sedum – *Hylotelephium spectabile* 'Autumn Joy' / White Japanese anemone – *Anemone x hybrida* 'White Knight' / Claret ash – *Fraxinus oxycarpa* 'Raywoodii' / Nigella (commonly known as love-in-a-mist) – *Nigella sativa* / Rosemary – *Salvia rosmarinus* / White lupin – *Lupinus mutabilis var. cruckshankii* 'White Javelin' / Coral-coloured penstemon – *Penstemon barbatus* 'Twizzle Coral' / Bog sage – *Salvia uliginosa*.

# PRECIOUS SPECIMENS

Surely the gateway to bringing plants indoors has always been the 'snip-at-speed' method. The moment your eye is caught by a solitary little specimen, whose beauty makes you pause, unable to resist bringing it with you to sit beside your desk/bed/bath or kitchen sink. Single stems in bud vases and bottles feel unpretentious and are a lovely little signal of the season.

Self-seeded, single-petal dahlia – unknown

Pansy – Viola x wittrockiana 'Delta Lavender Rose' Mix

Alpine strawberry – Fragaria vesca

Fading pink rose – Rosa 'West Coast'

Chrysanthemum 'Bronze'

Chrysanthemum 'Pink Alexis'

Bright pink zinnia – Zinnia elegans
'Giant Carmine Rose'

# PUMPKIN CURRY

## AND A PINT

There is nothing quite like a limited palette to really break the boundaries of what can go in a vase! While looking after my nieces at my sister's place, I decided to harvest everything I could scavenge from her garden, including her generous vege patch. I simply love the novelty of the sticky, apple-green hops, the twisted kōwhai and trumpets of pumpkin flowers! It's fair to say the pumpkin blooms didn't last more than a day in the vase, but despite this, they were worth the addition. The rest were a ragtag collection of odds and ends still in flower. Little yellow curry flowers, occasional handsome dahlias, the funny pompoms of monarda, combined with some blousy, beautiful old-fashioned roses.

*I began with the floppy stems of hops to see how they would sit, followed with kōwhai which can support*

*…many stems were quite short, hence the central grouping…*

other delicate stems. Roses are snipped to length, then again vertically up the stem to aid hydration...

...the kōhwai helped balance the shape of the arrangment in relation to the size of the vase.

Monarda

Rose

Scabiosa

Echinacea

Kōwhai

Rose

Curry
flower

Hops

Pumpkin
flower

Dahlia

*Common mint*

# PUMPKIN CURRY AND A PINT

Hops – *Humulus lupulus* / Pumpkin flower – *Cucurbita pepo* / Prostrate kōwhai – *Sophora prostrata* / Curry flower – *Helichrysum italicum* / Monarda (commonly known as bee balm) – *Monarda citriodora* 'Lemon Mint' / Common mint – *Mentha* / White echinacea – *Echinacea purpurea* 'Baby Swan White' / Pink scabiosa – *Scabiosa atropurpurea* 'Salmon Rose' / Self-seeded dahlia – *unknown* / White rose – *Rosa* 'Iceberg' / Other old-fashioned roses – *unknown*.

# LOVE LETTER

Calm greens, creamy petals, ruffles of blush and glowing accents make this messy little arrangement romantic and calm. Created quite quickly in an old glass bottle, it's a celebration of simple, classic tones with an unkempt edge. In particular I love that giant pretty face of my favourite dahila, 'Shiloh Noelle' and the smooth tips of my neighbour's honeysuckle that I have slowly trained over my side of the fence. As always, I'm drawn to sporadic mixes of flowers. The more the merrier and any bloom I can find is welcome, doing away with the need of formal balance.

Dahlia

Honeysuckle

Scabiosa

Fennel

Rose

Japanese
anemone

Aster

Hydrangea

Cosmos

Lupin

Astrantia

Dahlia

Clematis

# LOVE LETTER

Decorative dahlia – *Dahlia* 'Shiloh Noelle' / Self-seeded white single-petal dahlia – *unknown* / White decorative dahlia – *Dahlia* 'White Aster' / White pompom dahlia – *Dahlia* 'Petra's Wedding' / White Japanese anemone – *Anemone x hybrida* 'White Knight' / Japanese honeysuckle – *Lonicera japonica* / Cosmos – *Cosmos bipinnatus* 'Cupcake' / White lupin – *Lupinus mutabilis var. cruckshankii* 'White Javelin' / Astrantia (commonly known as masterwort) – *Astrantia major* 'Star Bush' / White rose – *Rosa* 'Iceberg' / Aster (commonly known as Michaelmas daisy) – *Aster salignus* / White lacecap hydrangea – *Hydrangea macrophylla var. normalis* / Common fennel – *Foeniculum vulgare* / Old man's beard (noxious weed creeping through my neighbour's fence!) – *Clematis vitalba* / White scabiosa – *Scabiosa caucasica* 'Fama White'.

# RUBIES & RASPBERRIES

Feeling inspired by my new vase purchased from New Zealand maker Pip Woods, I went out into the garden focused on a strong palette of bright green, jewel reds, blues and creamy whites. I arrived back inside with clutches of cosmos, scabiosa, jagged raspberry foliage with berries still attached and a scattering of bog sage amongst others. As always I love the mix of tiny starry blooms with big bold petals, resting in a nest of foliage and fruit. What's not to love, really?

Raspberry foliage

Aster

Bog sage

Delphinium

Astrantia

Scabiosa

Scabiosa

Lupin

Honeysuckle

Parsley flower

Rose

Aquilegia foliage

Cosmos

Raspberry

Tonka the cat

Vase by Pip Woods

*Honeysuckle is the gift that keeps giving, available for picking from late spring through to autumn.*

# RUBIES & RASPBERRIES

Burgundy cosmos – *Cosmos bipinnatus* 'Rubenza' / Raspberry – *Rubus idaeus* 'Aspiring' / Pacific giant delphinium – *Delphinium elatum* / Bog sage – *Salvia uliginosa* / White lupin – *Lupinus mutabilis var. cruckshankii* 'White Javelin' / Japanese honeysuckle – *Lonicera japonica* / Aster (commonly known as Michaelmas daisy) – *Aster salignus* / Dark scabiosa – *Scabiosa atropurpurea* 'Black Knight' / Creamy scabiosa – *Scabiosa ochroleuca* 'Lemon Scabiosa' / White rose – *Rosa* 'Iceberg' / Astrantia (commonly known as masterwort) – *Astrantia major* 'Star Bush' / Self-seeded aquilegia (commonly known as granny's bonnet or columbine) – *Aquilegia vulgaris* / Garden parsley – *Petroselinum crispum.*

# CRACKLE & POP

As the season slows, I move from a focus on blooms to a spotlight on shapes. Suddenly I can see the starry tips of young rosehips, the orange blush as they ripen and the sweet, earnest effort of the Icebergs still attempting to bud up. Lacecap hydrangeas become prized for their support as do my neighbour's electric-pink hebes peeping around the fence. This arrangement was the last hurrah of my ruby cosmos and the first showing of my very, very late flowering zinnias.

·

I nestled them all into a ceramic pot (very handy if you can find plant pots with no holes in the bottom!), supported in taped-down chicken wire for a very textural and poppy kitchen table arrangement.

Scabiosa

Rose

Zinnia

Hydrangea

Scabiosa

Rosehips

Honeysuckle

Cosmos

Parsley
flower

Hebe

# CRACKLE & POP

Bright pink zinnia – *Zinnia elegans* 'Giant Carmine Rose' / Dark scabiosa – *Scabiosa atropurpurea* 'Black Knight' / Garden parsley – *Petroselinum crispum* / White lacecap hydrangea – *Hydrangea macrophylla var. normalis* / White rose – *Rosa* 'Iceberg' / Burgundy cosmos – *Cosmos bipinnatus* 'Rubenza' / Magenta hebe – *Hebe speciosa* 'Magenta' / Japanese honeysuckle – *Lonicera japonica*.

# TAKE A LEAF

While autumn slowly steals away the blooms, it does generously replace them with other treasures fit for the vase. Aside from the obvious flaming colour, there are crab apples, pears, acorns, chestnuts, rosehips and seed heads galore. Always consider the shape of the tree or plant that you'll leave behind when harvesting, and use secateurs for nice clean cuts!

A crispy still life will last for weeks and certainly helps add to the seasonal nesting in any home.

Oak branches

Weeping pear

Rosehips

A mixed arrangement of autumn leaves and
seed heads from my garden.

Crab apple

Chestnuts

# WINTER

For years, my life gravitated around winter and the ski season. Waiting for snow, working on snow, travelling for snow, and living in sub-standard, freezing homes in ski towns with little thought of gardens or flowers.

Unlike the Northern Hemisphere, even in the deep south of New Zealand it would be unusual to have snow on the ground around our homes for any length of time. Where I live now, this just means it's cold; sometimes frosty, sometimes wet, and scavenging for joy for a vase becomes a challenge.

Winter is the season when most of our exciting blooms are over or dormant, leaving a subdued moment in the garden that feels like a distinct pause. Perennials have cosied back to their roots, trees have shut their eyes and shrubs stand guard around them.

Within this sense of still, in the misty crispness of brighter mornings, you can still find signs of life and beauty that can be collected to enjoy inside. The tangerine of my neighbour's japonica peeping over the fence, the ugly/pretty of outrageously fragrant wintersweet pinched for my office, and violets peeping up from the depths. Vivid red bottlebrush, catkins, otherworldly banksia dripping from giant trees and the excitement of the elegant hellebores beginning their bloom.

Soon after, the early narcissi and delicious daphne arrive with the keen pink tips of jasmine, snowdrops then snowflakes filing in. Aquilegia start to bolster their foliage and the first signs of blossom promise a treat with their maturing glossy buds.

Where I used to feel sad about my tonal winter garden and roadsides, I now realise there are always treasures to be found no matter what the season.

**Previous page:** My hallway becomes my studio, making the most of the mid-morning filtered light. 'The Great Gilroys' (page 132) stand to attention, ready for their portrait session. **Above:** 'Crowning Glory' (page 176) in a Tamara Rookes vessel, keeping my collection of finds company.

## My favourite winter pickings

HELLEBORES • WINTERSWEET • JAPONICA • NARCISSI • CATKINS • BOTTLEBRUSH • SNOWBERRY • DAPHNE • BANKSIA • MAGNOLIAS • SNOWDROPS • SNOWFLAKES • CAMELLIAS • VIOLETS • DAFFODILS • HEBE • PROTEAS • AUTUMN/WINTER BLOSSOMING PRUNUS • FORCED BLOSSOM AND SPRING GROWTH • SEED HEADS • JASMINE • PAPER DAISIES • ROSEMARY

# SWEETNESS OF WINTER

Most of what I find to pick in the depths of the winter months tends to be a little 'twiggy', the resulting arrangements a funny mix of hard and soft. When gathering branches of shrubs and trees, I try to harvest smartly, using sharp strong secateurs to make clean cuts and always considering the shape of the plant before I remove a limb.

·

Woody stems, like those of wintersweet and my early flowering cherry, need some special treatment for arranging. Make a 45-degree angular cut at the base of the stem followed by a second 'splitting' cut running up it vertically. This aids hydration and achieves a longer vase life.

·

Using a sweet little vase created by New Zealand maker Samantha Elise, I made a small, curled cushion of chicken wire, making sure I had trimmed any nodes or spikes from the branches that might get caught while threading into it. As the blossom was my most plentiful plant, I used this first to map out my shape and find my balance with the vessel size. I then poked in the precious few pieces of wintersweet and brittle limbs dripping catkins and cones of a black alder.

I curled up a square of chicken wire to make a pillow, fitting it snuggly in the vase...

...after trimming to length, I made a vertical cut up the stem to aid hydration...

*...I used my most plentiful stems of blossom to map out an assymetrical, scale-appropriate shape...*

*...I gently added in my few stems of winter sweet to fill the centre of the arrangement...*

*...catkins were spread at different heights to try and achieve balance.*

Cherry blossom

Wintersweet (foraged)

Black alder (foraged)

Vase by Samantha Elise

# SWEETNESS OF WINTER

Wintersweet – *Chimonanthus praecox* / Ornamental cherry blossom (commonly known as Higan Cherry) – *Prunus x subhirtella* 'Autumnalis Rosea' / Catkins and cones from the black alder tree – *Alnus glutinosa*.

# CROWNING GLORY

Of all the arrangements and experiments in this book, this took some reaching for. My garden was done, totally asleep, bar a desperate and surprised echinacea flower who wanted to be cut back, and premature hellebores teasing me with their floppy heads. I had recently bought this coveted vessel by New Zealand maker Tamara Rookes and imagined creating a huge head of 'hair' for it.

·

I hung around my untidied Japanese anemones, marvelling at their final seasonal stage, their little bobble seed heads cracking open to push out cotton wool balls of tiny seed. They were as exquisite as they were unusual. A 90-degree turn had me looking squarely at the silver-backed leaves of my feijoas, leaving no question what the mix would be.

·

Mapping the shape using feijoa branches supported by chicken wire, I then threaded in the delicate stems of Japanese anemone.

Japanese anemone
seed heads

Feijoa foliage

Vase by Tamara Rookes

*The seed heads burst as they mature.*

# CROWNING GLORY

Pink Japanese anemone – *Anemone x hybrida* 'Richard Ahrens' / Feijoa – *Acca sellowiana* 'Opal Star'.

# A DELICACY

For me, japonica is the real hero of July in Canterbury. Commonly called flowering quince, I have stuck with its old-fashioned moniker, feeling that it sounds as luxurious as it looks. Whether it be the silky tangerine blooms peeping over the fence directly in line with my office window, or the towering shrubs of pale pink and white that I visit in the depths of public space in my neighbourhood, to me it is simply romantic.

It is a terrific plant to collect while still only in bud so as to witness the gentle opening in the warmth of the house. Not long after, a closer look will reveal the ripening glossy buds on the bare branches of fruiting trees too! Wait patiently until they look plump then selectively and cleanly cut branches to suit, remembering that every bud presents fruit that you are sacrificing. It's a good idea to avoid harvesting while the tree is wet to avoid any possibility of disease entering the cut.

Condition your stems for the vase by making a 45-degree angular cut followed by a vertical slice up the branch to aid hydration. Remove any buds that might sit below the water level in your vessel.

Sit back and notice the slow, beautiful emergence of your blossom. Even once these flowers open and fade you will continue to enjoy the arrival of their bright spring leaves, making these arrangements points of interest for weeks on end!

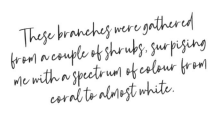

These branches were gathered from a couple of shrubs, surpising me with a spectrum of colour from coral to almost white.

# REFLECTIONS

As a mid-winter baby, my birthday cakes were always decorated with winter roses (hellebores). This was a tradition put in place by my mum and now, as a gardener, they feel like a connection to my childhood.

·

I made this soft, floaty arrangement on my 40th birthday. While I am a super sentimental and reflective person by nature, this birthday felt particularly like the beginning of a new chapter. It wasn't so much the big round number, but more the recent decision my husband and I had made to move on from our years of trying for a baby. Our focus now on being a happy twosome and exploring the silver linings in that.

·

While wrangling the fragrant tendrils of jasmine and experimenting with both scoring and searing different stems of hellebores, I let my mind wander through the pleasure and opportunity my garden has offered me. A place of distraction, a leafy corner for a cry and somewhere to dismiss intense disappointment by getting my hands busy. My own little patch of ground that has cultivated the expansion of my writing, photography and creative ideas. At this point in my life, I am most certain my garden holds the keys to both my personal comfort and career opportunities.

·

Built in an old silver footed vase with open neck and stuffed with a ball of chicken wire, I began with the floppy jasmine. After positioning these stems around the edge, I trimmed the hellebores, narcissi and snowflakes to different lengths to find the nostalgic, unfussy feeling I was looking for.

Narcissus

Hellebore

Snowflake

Jasmine

Rosemary

# REFLECTIONS

Hellebore (commonly known as winter rose) – *Helleborus orientalis* 'Pukehou Hybrids' and *Helleborus orientalis* 'Molly's White' / Common jasmine (which can be quite weedy!) – *Jasminum polyanthum* / Creamy and fragrant narcissus – *Narcissus* 'Erlicheer' / Snowflake – *Leucojum vernum* 'Spring snowflake' / Rosemary – *Rosmarinus prostratus.*

# FRESH BREATH

Daffodils work hard to deliver and delight us with sunny promises of spring, often while winter still has a grip. This arrangement presents the traditional winter treasures of hellebores, camellias and snowflakes with trumpeting daffs, creamy narcissi, blousy cherry blossom and my year-round-fruiting limequat.

•

When gathering these plants together, there is some particular prep required. Narcissi and daffodils should be trimmed to estimated length and set apart from other plants to hydrate in water to dispel their sap and seal. As hellebores can be so disappointing to harvest with their intent to flop and wilt, get ahead by gathering stems of flowers that have at least one bloom with a developed central seed pod; this will make all the difference. Trim to length and sear the bottom 10 per cent of the stem in freshly boiled water for 20–30 seconds before putting into the cool water of a vase. Another option is to skip the searing and instead score down the lower half of the stem using a sharp blade, opening it ever so slightly to allow more water in.

•

Camellias and limequat limbs ask for a clean 45-degree trim to size followed by a second, vertical slicing cut up the stem. This helps hugely with hydration.

•

As with all my arrangements of this size, they are made easy by the support of a pillow of chicken wire and pot tape to secure.

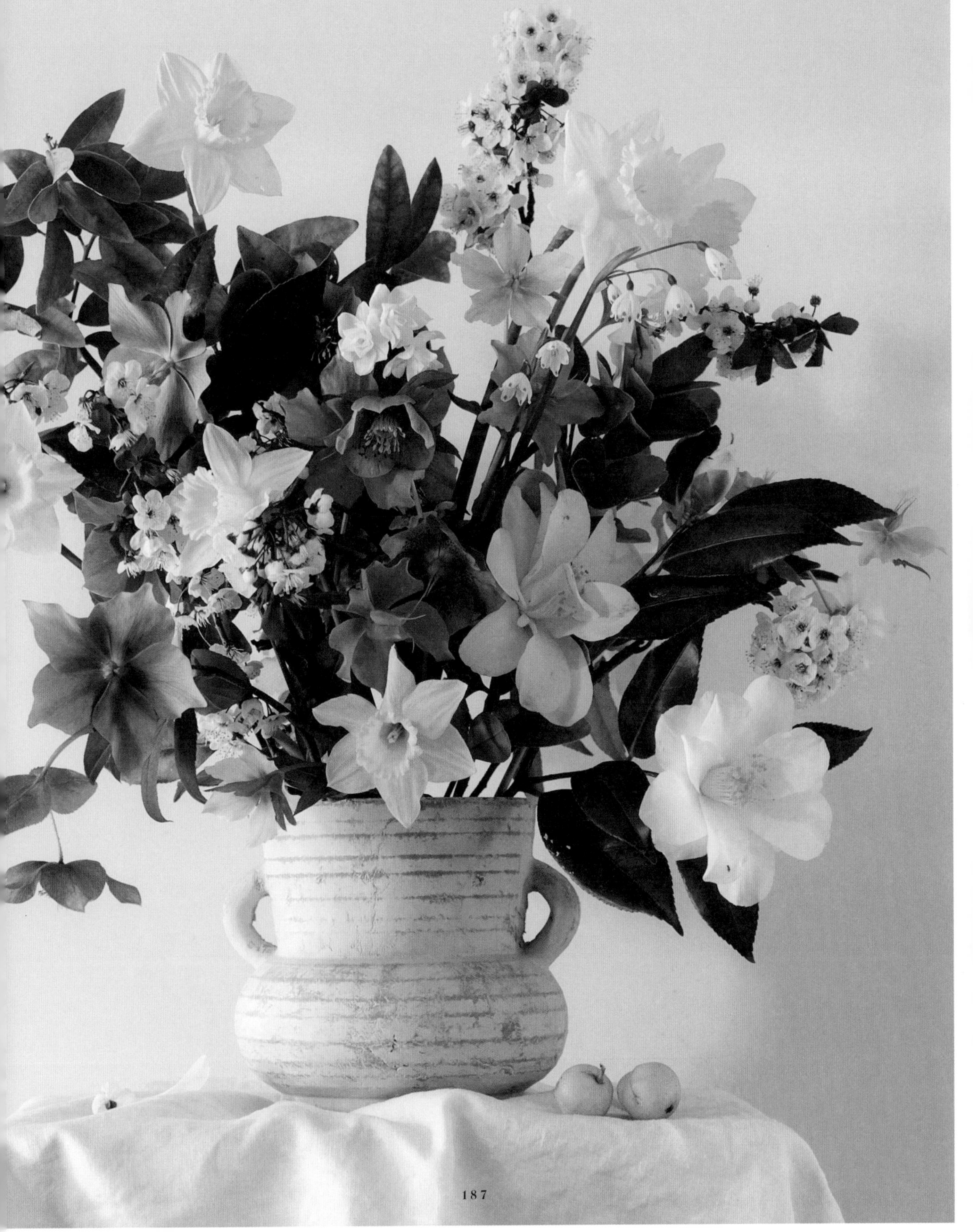

Plum
blossom

Daffodil

Narcissus

Hellebore

Limequat

Snowflake

Daffodil

Hellebore

Camellia

# FRESH BREATH

Hellebore (commonly known as winter rose) – *Helleborus orientalis* 'Pukehou Hybrids' / Limequat – *Citrofortunella x floridana* 'Eustis' / Snowflake (commonly known as summer snowflake) – *Leucojum aestivum* / White camellia – *Camellia sasanqua* 'Setsugekka' / Large yellow daffodil – *Narcissus* 'Carlton' / Creamy and fragrant smaller narcissus – *Narcissus* 'Erlicheer' / Purple leaf plum – *Prunus cerasifera* / Daffodil with yellow trumpet and white petals – *Narcissus* 'Goblet'.

# Flowers
# for Friends

### JULIA ATKINSON-DUNN

KOA PRESS

Published in 2021 by Koa Press Limited.

www.koapress.co.nz

Director: Tonia Shuttleworth
Editor: Lucinda Diack
Sub-editor: Belinda O'Keefe
Designer: Tonia Shuttleworth
Photographer: Julia Atkinson-Dunn
Illustrator: Amy Jones, www.cheesebeforebedtime.art

ISBN 978-0-473-58768-0

Printed in China by 1010 Printing.

## Thank you

I am well aware that the process of bringing my books to life with
Koa Press is not the same experience other creatives have with
larger publishing houses. The second time around has been as
intensely collaborative and enjoyable as our first, building on our
shared vision as much as our friendship. I value and feel so lucky to
have my work transformed by both Tonia's design skills, great taste
and constant flow of tasty cheds which we nibbled on nonstop,
sitting side by side at the computer. I can never thank her enough!!

A huge amount of gratitude again goes to the editing team of
Lucinda Diack and Belinda O'Keefe who allow me to ramble when
necessary but are the backstop for my grammar gone astray and
important missing information!

This book really rests on the confidence and warmth I have felt
from my online audience. Their keen interest and positivity so
openly given when sharing my seasonal experiments encouraged
me to keep it up. I hope they find inspiration, knowledge and their
own passion for growing and playing with flowers too.

As always, Mum and Dad, Caroline and Simon, Ada and Rosella are
my main gang of supporters whom I'd be lost without.

My darling T is the tree who holds everything up.
Xoxo

Julia Atkinson-Dunn
www.studiohome.co.nz / @studiohomegardening / @studiohome